BREAKING ALL THE RULES

How the #1 Female Earner in

Network Marketing Rose to The Top

JENNA ZWAGIL

LEGAL DISCLAIMER:

Published by

Success in 100 Pages

www.SuccessIn100Pages.com

ISBN 978-1-947814-60-8

"If you obey all the rules, you miss all the fun."

— Katharine Hepburn

DEDICATION

To my husband Josh, and my children: Evan, Troy, Zoë, and Ari.

Without their love and support, none of this
would have been possible.

TABLE OF CONTENTS

FOREWORD by
Bob Proctor

I believe this book will change the lives of a lot of people.

There's something in here for everyone. You can be one of the most successful people in town, you'll love this book. The honesty and direct approach to problems we all face from time to time is refreshing. You'll gain the confidence from Jenna, that whatever's going on you can make it better.

It's definitely going to create hope in the mind of many who have been struggling for so long.

There are a great number of people who seem as if they have lost hope. They've struggled for so long and have simply given up. If this resonates with you or you're looking for something different, listen up. As Jenna Zwagil begins to share her story, you are going to be filled with hope. This book will illuminate a light within you that perhaps has been hidden, that you couldn't see. That's what hope does—it gives us options.

Jenna shares many wonderful lessons in *Breaking All the Rules*. Jenna is the epitome of success that so many young people dream about. But it wasn't always like that for Jenna.

When I first met Jenna, I noticed something right away. She has a quality that almost every living soul looks for or wants to develop. Jenna is in control of Jenna. She has developed an awareness that if you want something, you can have it. It's an awareness and understanding that only comes from study. She's truly transparent in sharing how she has become such a tremendous success sharing both the bad and the good.

Jenna has developed herself into a strong, accomplished individual. In this book, *Breaking All the Rules*, she takes you on a page-by-page journey of how she went from being truly broke to very wealthy. Her life has definitely not been a walk in the park. She describes the hang ups she had, but through study she learned how to overcome them, to work her way through the problems to enjoy success. Where most would have given up, she kept going. The beautiful part is that Jenna shares how she did it so clearly that the reader can learn from her shortcomings and triumphs.

I have been around network marketing since it began over 50 years ago. I have a very mature business but every now and then someone asks me if I was starting over, what would I do? Without hesitation, I tell them I would become a network marketer. I truly believe it's one of the greatest opportunities that has developed in my lifetime.

Go back in history as far as you can go, clear back to the ancient Babylonians, and you will find that all wealthy people have had multiple sources of income. That's one of the great secrets of financial success. It should be taught to us as children, but it's not. Fortunately, it's been built into the network marketing industry. It has nothing to do with your past, with what you have done, with where you have been, with how you've struggled. It focuses on one thing: what you do NOW.

This book is a Godsend for those searching for that illusive something—something better, something bigger, something different—whether you're in network marketing or not. There are no flashy strategies, you don't need an MBA in business to understand it, but like Jenna, you must believe in you. If you don't, I guarantee she will help you in this area. She definitely didn't start out believing in herself and she's not a free-wheeling single young lady, although she is young.

Jenna and her husband, Josh, have built a $100M company in a relatively short period of time. You would like the both of them. They're really good people. They're not only building a big company, but they're also raising a young family, they have 4 children. There's an old saying, if you want something done, give it to a busy person. Jenna gets it done. She's the Chief Marketing Officer of their company.

If you want to be free, truly free in today's world, you must have a respectable income. Network marketing gives everyone, regardless of their past, an opportunity to become financially independent. The fact that only a small percentage accomplish that, is another thing.

Jenna is one of the winners, in fact, one of the biggest earners, if not the biggest, in network marketing worldwide. In the pages of this book, she tells you how she's done it. And she tells it in such a way that you will see how you, too, can do it. That's Jenna's sole reason for writing this book.

Bob Proctor
Best-selling author, *You Were Born Rich*

Preface:

I t felt like a dream, sitting backstage watching the TV monitors, waiting to be introduced for my speech to thousands of people from all over the world who came to attend our annual convention.

Our company was growing at an incredible pace. The product line we'd launched in May 2017 brought in $9.7 million that first year, then revenue grew a thousand percent in 2018, generating $100 million in sales. For the present year, we were forecasting $170 million, having attracted hundreds of thousands of affiliates and customers.

Almost every convention speech I've given has been about vision, training, skills, and mindset. This time it was different. This time I was sharing my story.

The thing is, my story isn't really my story anymore—I no longer identify with who I used to be, only who I've become in the process. I credit much of these changes to the challenges I was faced with, and the people along the way who made everything possible.

As I heard my introduction coming over the loudspeakers, I realized that my moment had finally arrived. It was such a long journey to get here, and now I was finally on the other side. Now it was time to share my story so the audience could have the courage to change theirs. I changed my story through my willingness to break the rules.

*"If you're always trying to be normal you will
never know how amazing you can be."*

-Maya Angelou

CHAPTER I:

Forget the Rules

When I set out to be a network marketer, I was told I had to change who I was to become successful. I was told I had to dress up and attend hotel meetings, I had to speak and act like a professional, and that social media should only be used to promote the business and never, ever be used to discuss politics, religion, cannabis, vaccines or for that matter anything controversial.

I wanted to become successful, but I also wanted to stay true to myself. I couldn't imagine a life of influencer puppetry, where the almighty dollar was priority over creating world change. I didn't get into this industry for just a paycheck. I wanted to create impact: a ripple effect of positivity throughout the cosmos. I wanted to prove to the world that it is possible to be uniquely you, with a voice, and also become wildly successful.

I'm here to tell you that anyone who has ever said you had to sell out to become great was wrong. Maybe that is how they got there, but that is not the only way. The days of "fake it till you make it" are over. Image isn't everything, and the number-one thing people are seeking out in today's leadership is transparency.

Success isn't reserved just for *those* people, the polished ones, the society-addicted boujee-types, or the egocentric know-it-all-about-everything ones. You can just be you and still create massive success.

People say my story sounds like a movie. In many ways, it is. It starts with someone lost in the wilderness, wandering, just trying to survive.

The next act includes a quest for health, wealth, and happiness. But like in most movies, the plot thickens before it resolves. There are roadblocks along the way that show up to challenge you. Breaking through will require a desire for growth and a willingness to persevere against all odds.

Finally, it's a success story. The happy ending.

I suppose you could say I am successful. I've earned a million dollars per month and became the #1 female income earner in the network marketing industry. By most people's standards, that would be considered hugely successful. Success to me isn't just reaching that goal paycheck though—it's impact, it's legacy, it's the way people remember you when you're gone. This is my definition of success, and by *that*, I am still working toward it.

Unlike the movies though, I didn't have to sell my soul to the devil or join the Illuminati to become successful either. I was able to reach success while keeping my integrity, mission, faith, and sanity intact.

I didn't follow society's or my parents' rules for success and succeeded anyway. I'm here to tell you that success is not only possible but also your birthright.

I've Always Been a Rule Breaker

From an early age I was a rule breaker, which is not the same as being a law breaker. Well, mostly not. Like many people, I occasionally break the law, especially stupid laws that hurt no one. Like jaywalking when there are no cars in sight or smoking weed in a state that hasn't caught up with the times. But this book isn't about breaking laws; it's about breaking rules.

Rule:
Success is for a certain type of person.

Reality:
Success is for anyone willing to conquer their fears.

There's a big difference.

Breaking laws, even if they're stupid, can get you fined, fired, or thrown in the back of a cop car. If the law is big enough, it might even land you in prison. Sadly, the majority of laws are outdated, absurd and unjust.

In Nevada, where I live, it is illegal to conceal a spray-painted shopping cart in your basement. In Arizona, it is illegal to let a donkey sleep in your bathtub, and in Baltimore it's illegal to swear within the city limits. I lived in Baltimore and I can tell you first-hand that every jail cell would be full if police arrested one tenth of the people who ignored this one.

Admittedly, rules do serve a purpose. It's just rarely *your* purpose—it's someone else's. Nine out of 10 times, the rules we follow only prevent us from achieving our potential. They steal our futures and rob us of our individuality.

They also keep us poor.

This is why I believe rules are made to be broken—especially if the goal is to lead an extraordinary life.

Some Rules <u>Are</u> Helpful

Now, admittedly, there are rules that most of us find helpful. Like, obviously, rules that ensure physical safety: look both ways before crossing the street; don't eat food way past the expiration date; don't swim in an area where there are riptide warnings all over the place; hanging off the railing at the edge of the Grand Canyon to take an Instagram selfie is probably not a good idea either. Life is way too precious to spend it doing things to impress people who don't care, anyway.

And then there are some rules and laws designed to promote morality: don't lie, don't cheat, don't steal, don't murder, etc. Things like that.

I'm in favor of many rules of morality, but not for religious or societal reasons. I'm in favor of them because I'm a big believer in karma. The Law of Compensation (Karma) is one of the laws of the universe. It's as certain as the law of gravity. What goes up, must come down. What goes around *does* come around. You will reap what you sow. Maybe not tomorrow or even in this lifetime, but rules of morality that are broken today *will* come back to bite you somewhere down the road. For instance, all the waffles and carbs I ate in my twenties, when there was no repercussion to what I ate, is karmically now showing up in my thirties.

I'm also in favor of rules that create good habits, like morning and nighttime routines. Making your bed, brushing your teeth, reading personal development books every day, and not eating too many waffles. Rules like that make sense.

But rule-making can become a slippery slope. One day you're following rules that make your life better, and next thing you know, you're following rules that make no difference. Then, you're following rules that are just plain destructive.

To me, the fewer the rules you have in your life, the better. But the rest—rules that keep you from living your dreams? These were not only made to be ignored—they were made to be broken.

I Don't Really Break Every Rule

Obviously, I don't break *every* rule. I do follow the ones that are helpful in achieving my goals and dreams. And I follow laws that make sense. But I never blindly *obey* them.

Rule:
To be a good person, you must follow the rules.

Reality:
You can still be a good person and also think for yourself.

To me, *obey* is a four-letter word. To "obey" is to comply with a command, to submit to the authority. *I never obey without question.*

Most rules are created by people in positions of power for the sole purpose of keeping themselves in power.

I take any rule created with the intent of ensuring my obedience by restricting my liberty as a personal threat. The same goes for any rule forced on people by society that stifles creativity, destroys individuality, or reduce a person's chances at success.

My three "rules about following rules" are:

1. Never follow any rule without questioning it first.

2. Never follow rules that limit you negatively, only rules that empower you.

3. Never accept a rule as unchangeable just because others blindly follow.

History tells us that any rule that restricts freedom and discourages self-sufficiency must eventually be challenged and broken. The human spirt guarantees it.

The majority of rules (and laws) we are forced to follow were created with good intentions and almost always in the name of safety. Ah, safety—the thing most people seek, and the thing that dooms us to an average life, all in one word.

So many rules passed down—with good intentions, for the most part—lead us to be timid, fearful and poor.

Written vs. Unwritten Rules

The rules I've broken in my life are mostly of the unwritten variety—things that are passed down verbally, by friends, family, and society in general. The reason they're unwritten is because if we actually saw them in writing, it would become immediately obvious how ridiculous they are. These include:

You *should* go to college...

You *should* get a good job with a big company...

You *should* work hard and keep your head down...

You *should* buy a house...

You *should* get married and stay married...

You *should* buy insurance, save for a rainy day, and retire at age 65 with enough money to not end up homeless in your 80s.

When someone says, *"Take my advice, you should...,"* what they are really doing is sharing one of the rules *they've* formed for *their* life, so you should be afraid to break them, too. When we go along with what we're told we *should* do, we end up "*shoulding*" on ourselves a lot. If you don't want to live their life, you shouldn't take their advice. Plain and simple.

Should 'Normal' Be the Goal?

Most rules aren't really even rules—*they're expectations.* They are the things society expects us to do, things people have come to accept as safe, reasonable, normal.

People love being normal because they fear being thought of as different. I'm all in on different. Different is outside the norm. Different is unique. Different is, well, *different.*

When I was a kid, I can honestly say I did not want to be like the cool kids in school. I always thought it was strange that the goal was to impress other people and act and be like everyone else. What was the point of that? What a waste of creative energy. I wondered if this is how it was in the real world too, or if this human behavior only existed at school.

I was never bullied for being different either. I never let others' opinions bother me. I knew who I was, and I embraced it. I was a band nerd, a poet, and an ASB spirit commissioner. I was so secure in myself I didn't bother with what everyone else was doing. That seemed like a waste of time when I could be off doing my own thing or hanging out with other kids who were also not that cool but exponentially more interesting.

To be normal is to be average. The exceptional people in the world are *exceptions* to the norm. Normal is a trap. I'll take different every time.

I've come to understand that being different isn't bad—it's better. Different is unique. Different is noticeable. Different is fascinating. Different is smart. People who are different are usually more creative, more caring, and more daring. Different is making an impression and having impact on the world.

Normal people keep their heads down. Normal people don't make waves. They follow the rules and don't question them. They do everything they can to avoid standing out. They follow the herd, nose to tail. Being in the herd feels safe—at least until you get to the slaughter chute.

Normal people take actions that conform to what the majority is doing; rule breakers beat their own path.

Normal people aim for safety; rule breakers aim for excellence.

Normal people have good relationships; rule breakers demand exciting, loving and fulfilling relationships.

Normal people work really hard to fit in; rule breakers understand that no one is quite like them, which makes them not only unique but makes them irreplaceable.

Make Your Own Rules

What rules do *you* want to live by? Once you decide you are going to take control of your life, there is only yourself to stop you. Life is too short to play it safe and by other people's expectations. No one ever became great by doing what everyone else is doing.

The people who become extraordinary do so by stepping out of the crowd and into their full potential.

This book is about how I broke the rules to achieve everything I wanted in my life. You'll learn the exact steps I took to do it so you, too, can create the life of your dreams.

"We are never trapped unless we choose to be."
-Anis Nin

CHAPTER II:
Trapped Between Two Worlds

Like many kids, I rebelled and questioned my parents. They divorced when I was six months old and remarried other people shortly after. I never grew up in one place. Two homes is all I ever knew.

Rule:
There are many reasons why people fail.

Reality:
The majority of 'reasons' are really 'excuses.'

At my dad's house, I was "Jenny." Jenny was the only sister to three older brothers. For the majority of my life, I only visited on weekends and a couple weeks in the summer. My whole early life was court dates over custody. My dad and stepmom tried to get custody of me while my mom defended her position as primary parent until I turned 12 and was allowed to choose where I wanted to live. At that point, I chose to live with my dad until I was 17.

I thought that by moving to his house I'd have the opportunity to get to know him. I was wrong. The week I moved in, my oldest brother got into a drinking-and-driving accident. He was 16 years old and his best friend who was sitting in the passenger seat experienced brain damage from the accident. His parents sued my parents, and the financial loss that occurred thereafter changed the whole family vibe. We were raised in the church but stopped going when the church turned its back on us. All at once, the light-hearted, happy place I used to visit became very dark, very fast. Suddenly they were drinking more, laughing less and I became invisible.

Everybody was living their own lives and I wasn't sure where I fit in. I was late to the party. I didn't know the inside jokes. I didn't have the same rules as them at my mom's. I was constantly at odds, navigating choppy waters in foreign seas.

Because my experience with them was limited, I wasn't sure I could fully trust them. It was difficult to have a relationship with my dad when he was stressed and mentally preoccupied. There were times when I felt he was truly present and other times, checked out. Raising four teenagers at once is no easy feat, and I know they did the best they could.

It wasn't until later in life as a young adult that I finally did connect with him. We had a lot in common and were finally able to communicate. It was the first time I felt I had a place in his life, which is why it took me by surprise when he told me he could no longer speak to me. His last words to me were that "he loved me, that I was strong, and that I would be fine." That was it.

For seven years he ignored all my calls, texts, letters in the mail and refused to acknowledge my existence. It wasn't just him though. It was my entire family. I went from two families to one, overnight.

My Other World

My mom's world was the exact opposite. Here, I was called "Jennifer" or "fur fur" by my younger siblings when they were babies. I was the oldest of 3 and had a younger sister and younger brother. My highest responsibility I felt growing up was setting a good example for them. I always felt compelled to do the right thing because I knew they were watching. Unfortunately, for most of my early adult life, the example I set was of what *not* to do.

When I was *Jennifer,* I was able to express myself. I was allowed to be weird and "goofy" was embraced. I felt accepted in this tribe, and as imperfect as it was, I felt home. I was encouraged to pursue my passions in music and in writing, and it was here that I learned it was okay to be different.

My mom was quirky, creative, and also hilarious. When she wasn't being funny though, she was reminiscing of her younger days when she still pursued her dream of being a singer. My mom was a great singer.

Watching her give up her dreams was the single most important reason why I didn't give up on mine.

I didn't want to have a "what if" life. What if I had followed my dreams? What if I hadn't given up? What if I had just gone for it? What if I stopped caring about what everyone told me who to be and what to do, and just simply followed my own heart? I wasn't afraid of risk—I was afraid to live with regret.

Living in two different worlds, with two different perspectives of what family was, what normal was, and what reality was, taught me to create life myself instead of accepting the imprints of someone else's creations. I learned early on that I did not want to be unfulfilled and unhappy. I knew I wanted more.

An Excuse for Self-Blame

Like many children are known to do, I used their divorce as a reason to not love myself. After all, if they didn't love me enough to stay together or even be cordial for my sake, then why should I? If my dad didn't feel I was worth sticking around for, then I must not have mattered that much. My self-worth was non-existent.

I've come to learn over the years that while our reasons explain why we do things, excuses are what hold us back. Excuses justify giving up.

"I would go to college except I don't have the money."

"I would start a business, but I don't have the time."

"I would follow my dreams except no one really makes it, so why bother?"

In every sense of my life, I was an excuse maker. I didn't take accountability for my lack of results. I was so good at making excuses, I actually *believed* them to be true.

What we don't realize is we are either creating consciously or subconsciously all the time. What we tell ourselves in our mind *is* what manifests in the physical. Truth or not. Positive or negative. Fact or fiction.

If you internalize a belief, you will act toward making it true in your life, even if it's not.

Welcome to Adulthood

I graduated high school with a 3.8 GPA. I was still under the impression that if I got good grades, I'd be able to go to a good college, and if I got into a good college I would automatically have a good career. Well, I got into the good college with my good grades, but I couldn't go. I didn't have the money and I couldn't get any student loans because I was still under my parents' responsibility (until age 26) even though I had moved out of their house.

So instead, I got married to a guy in my English class I had met my senior year. Just a few months after we got married, I was pregnant. A few months after that, he was deployed with the Marine Corps. I gave birth to my first son, Evan, during that deployment. I was 19. That was my introduction into adulthood. I was shocked into a state of survival with only two options: sink or swim.

I wasn't ready to be a mom yet, and the reality of it didn't hit me until after I had become one. Maybe it was being bipolar, maybe it was my own stupidity, but I had a knack for pushing the throttle in life just for the sake of it. Time and time again, I found myself in situations I couldn't get out of, but I'm not so sure I was meant to get *out* of them. In hindsight, I know I was meant to go *through* them.

Being a young mom taught me to grow up fast and that if this baby had to rely on me, I had better figure out how to rely on me, too. For the first six weeks of Evan's life, it was just me and him and countless, sleepless nights.

Evan's dad returned home from Iraq a changed man, but I had changed, too. After struggling to find common ground, we decided to end our marriage and go our separate ways.

Get a "Real Job"

After many false starts and a failed marriage under my belt, my mom encouraged me to get a "real job" to support myself. She had been through a divorce herself and knew how important it would be for me to fully support myself. Being a single mom left me with no choice anyway, so I took her advice.

I found a job at the cable company that started out paying $20/hour. This was a dream job for many people, but for me it felt like I had sold my soul for a paycheck. The thought of committing to a basic job for the sake of safety just didn't sit well with me. On top of that, it was a three-hour commute every day and I had to leave my then two-year-old son behind in daycare.

Rule:
Friends and family want what is best for you.

Reality:
Your friends and family want what's safe for you and best for them.

Within six months of working there, I became the #1 sales agent in the country and earned the "Rookie Award." It was a goal I set for myself in trying to spark some passion and stay committed. I got anxiety every time I had to punch a code in my phone when I wanted to use the restroom and when I had to rush back from lunch to clock in.

I knew deep down that this would never work for my spirit. I didn't yet realize that the spirit within me that kept me bouncing around to different jobs was actually my entrepreneurial spirit.

After eight months I was given two options: to quit or be fired. Even though I was their top sales agent, they were ready to let me go after discovering I had been dating my boss. Rules, again, broken.

Losing that job was somehow more real than all the others. I had planned to sell my soul to the clock-in machine after mustering up enough mental servitude to truly commit. I just never got there. I worried if I'd be able to get another job like that one but also questioned if I really wanted one or not. I was torn between this false sense of safety and true freedom. Deep down, I knew I was meant for more than trading my time for money.

Getting fired was probably the best thing that could have happened. It created discomfort. Discomfort meant I was exiting my comfort zone and forced to stretch once again. Humans, like rubber bands, are useless unless stretched. We can never reach our full potential if we are never stretched.

Being stretched means facing life's challenges head on and knowing those challenges are *for* you, not "in spite" of you.

You must learn from life's lessons to level up. You cannot go to the next level without mastering the one you're on. All of life is a lesson and I was learning them fast. I knew that there was probably no job worth keeping long-term. Working for someone else on someone else's goals was just not for me.

So, what did I do next? I joined the Army, the only job you can't quit and that forces people to take orders from authority.

Enlisting in the Army

With very few options available, and not being ready to pursue my dreams, the military seemed like a solid option.

I'll be honest, it wasn't my first choice. I had just been a Marine wife and knew the challenges of raising a child with only one parent available; but when the recruiter showed up offering a $20,000 bonus and a ticket out of town, I thought it was worth considering.

There weren't many jobs in the Army I was especially excited about, but Human Resources (42A) seemed like something I could do. To get this job, I needed to score a 52 on the ASVAB (Armed Services Vocational Aptitude Battery).

If I got a 50 or above, I would be able to get the job I wanted and the bonus; if I scored below a 50, there would be no bonus and I wouldn't be joining.

I scored a 52.

Soon after I got my test results, I was swearing in over the Bible to become a United States army solider. In many ways, my time in the military was an amazing experience, but it was also tough. I spent four years thinking, "This can't be it. There has to be another way to make a living and take back control of my life." There must be more to life than waking up to the sound of somebody else's orders.

History Repeats Itself

Once out of basic training, I got married again, this time to a solider I met in training. Soon after getting married, I became pregnant again with my son, Troy. Troy's dad and I were good friends but terrible as husband and wife. Our marriage ended after three years. We both transitioned out of the military, and he took a job in Baltimore and gained custody of our son. This became a motivating factor for my success. I wanted Troy in my life, and I didn't want money to stop me. I knew I had to become rich if I wanted to afford plane tickets, hotel stays, and maybe even a second home near him someday.

I was up for a new adventure and a new life. One thing I learned from these experiences is that if you want to change your life you have to take risks. Not all the risks I took worked out. But to me, it was better to risk and try than to never try at all and live with regret forever.

Growing up with two different perspectives of life gave me the insight to know that a new reality was only a decision away. I could change anything in my life with simply the intent to change it backed by massive action.

"We are not going in circles, we are going upward. The path is spiral; we have already climbed many steps."

-Hermann Hesse

CHAPTER III:

Running in Circles

I was exposed to network marketing for the first time when I was only 18. The company was called Quixtar, which I later discovered was technically Amway in disguise. It was a recruitment that had been several years in the making.

For much of my childhood, I played trumpet in the band. One of my friends, a fellow trumpet-player, was a kid named Daniel. After we'd graduated high school, Daniel invited me to a meeting at our old band teacher's house. He said he was making money without working a job, so I agreed to go.

The meeting set up was pretty simple. It was a few chairs in a circle and an easel with a pad of paper for the presentation. Mr. C welcomed us to his home with his wife and began drawing circles on the board in the shape of a pyramid. He talked about McDonald's, Ray Kroc, and the power of franchising, and how if you wanted to make money in your sleep, you needed to create leverage. Trading time for money was *"a trap,"* he said. It was a classic introduction to network marketing, but I remember sitting there, just 18 years young, thinking, "This sounds better than getting a job—maybe I'll try it."

I didn't *need* this opportunity, but I was intrigued by it. I still had the belief that the American Dream was real and there would be a high-paying job waiting for me at the end of the college rainbow.

I joined the business using my new credit card I got from the bank. I didn't have $500 saved for a new venture. I was sure I'd make the money back before the bill came in the mail, but I was wrong. I couldn't get anyone else to buy from me or join, so I didn't make my money back.

Because I made no money, I did what most inexperienced network marketers do when they hit their first roadblock—I quit.

Rule:
Failure teaches us what we're not good at.

Reality:
Failure teaches us what we need to become better at.

I decided network marketing must not work or at least not for me. The reality was no one wanted to join a broke college-aged kid with no business or life experience. Even the most gullible of prospects could see through my lack of understanding in this new venture. I didn't realize that my own life journey would become the testimony that would catapult my career in the next chapter of my life.

That first exposure planted a seed. Every time I found myself in a new job that wasn't working out, I'd wonder if maybe there was something more to being an entrepreneur. Maybe there was still a way I could actually make it work.

Second Brush With Network Marketing

In 2012, I encountered network marketing for the second time. The first time, I'd failed and quickly gave up. This time things were different. Now I had two boys, two mouths to feed. I needed to buy groceries and put food on the table. It wasn't just about me anymore. It was about taking care of Evan and Troy. I remember at Christmas wanting to buy gifts for my kids but having no money. I maxed out my credit cards, year after year, never paying them off fully from the year before. That was the cycle I was in.

Desperate to make more money, I joined a new company.

I was the type of networker who could hit the third or fourth rank easily. I had a sales background and recruiting came easily. I knew how to relate to people and find their need. Many people would join me but then they would quit, leaving me back to square one. After they would all quit, so would I. I figured they didn't like the products enough to stay or wanted success badly enough. It wasn't until much later in my network marketing career did I realize that people were quitting because of my lack of leadership.

I simply wasn't ready to become a professional in the industry and a student of self-development. Because of these reasons, I could not find success no matter what company I was in.

I had to do massive work on myself. I was still struggling with my past and suffering from massive self-worth issues. I didn't feel I deserved success even though I was trying desperately to achieve it. Every time I made even the slightest amount of progress, I let feelings of inadequacy and self-doubt get in the way.

The Network Marketing 'Bell'

There is a proverb that says, "you can't unring a bell." It means that once something is seen or heard, it can't be unseen or unheard. Just like learning to ride a bike, once you learn how, you can't make yourself forget. You can do your best to make the future better but *knowing* changes things. Knowledge has consequences.

My bell? Having seen the network marketing opportunity. As time passed and I went from job to job, I kept thinking, "Working a job is hard. Network marketing is hard. But at least with network marketing, there's a chance at freedom."

From that moment on, even when I was at my lowest in terms of self-esteem and struggling to survive, network marketing was always in the back of my mind. Especially since I kept taking sales jobs. If I could sell insurance, I could sell vitamins and other things from the comfort of my own home.

Yet knowing this, I still refused to make the commitment to make it happen. But why? The reason had nothing to do with the industry—*it had everything to do with me.*

I kind of dabbled in and out of the industry for about 10 years. I would have some success, and then I would let things slide back. I tried every company that you can probably think of in those years, blaming my lack of success on a long list of *maybes*:

Maybe the product is the problem.

Maybe it's my upline.

Maybe it's corporate leadership.

Maybe it's the compensation plan.

Maybe it's the reputation of the MLM industry.

Maybe it's whatever.

I used every maybe in the book for why it was impossible for me to succeed. Something had to change.

Everything Is Created Twice

One of my earliest introductions to the Law of Attraction was watching the movie "The Secret" when it came out in 2006. At first, I thought the whole idea that you could *manifest things with your mind* was all woo-woo and a bit out there. "Thoughts become things," Bob Proctor would say.

Rule:
Seeing is believing.

Reality:
**Believing is seeing.
Everything is created twice, once in the mind and then in physical reality.**

The Law of Attraction? Manifesting things with your mind? How? As far as I knew, things only existed in the physical world and nowhere else. I thought the physical world was the only world we had control of. I had no clue that my subconscious mind was the key player in my current life manifestations. I'd already manifested many things in my life. Unfortunately, the primary thing I'd manifested was poverty and failed relationships. Yes, thoughts *do* become things—*but they can also become the lack of things.*

The more I thought about it, it became obvious that everything is created twice, first in the mind, second in reality. Everything. There isn't a single thing created that wasn't an idea *before* it came into existence, from paper clips to skyscrapers to rocket ships.

According to Wallace D. Wattles in, "The Science of Getting Rich"—formally titled, "Financial Success through Creative Thought" and a book later given to me from the great, Bob Proctor himself—"We live in a thought world, which is part of a thought universe."

For those who want to go down the religious path, even the natural elements—rocks and trees and animals and water—all were created twice, too, once in the mind of God and once again in physical reality. "Let there be Light," says God, and then there was. The creation process within us is no different.

This book you are reading right now was first a thought. It was a thought I held in my mind for several years before it existed in physical reality. And as Bob Proctor declares, "If you can see it in your mind, you can hold it in your hand."

The question is, at what point did it become real? When I thought about writing it or when I wrote it?

The answer is both.

Accepting Responsibility

Most people don't want to deal with the truth about how they ended up where they are in life, the trap *they* allowed themselves to get caught in, what *they* allowed themselves to become. Looking in the mirror and knowing you let this happen to yourself is painful. This was the situation I found myself in.

The truth is a tough pill to swallow, which is why most people spit it out.

When I thought about my life, my story, and my circumstances, it was easy to blame my parents, my siblings, my ex-spouses, the media, the government, the cards I had been dealt, and on and on. But even though these external things had an impact on me, I needed to accept responsibility for my role in it.

Most of what I'd experienced in my life wasn't entirely my fault, but it was my responsibility for how I responded to it, how I internalized those events, how I interpreted them. The events didn't determine my situation, but my response to them did.

Whenever I'd been faced with the truth about myself, I did what everyone does. I looked for ways to escape. And I didn't need to go very far to find distractions.

Distractions are everywhere.

The world is one big collection of distractions—TV, food, alcohol, shopping, concerts, sporting events, etc., and my personal favorites up to that point—changing careers and changing homes. Every time I started feeling unhappy, I'd pivot to a new job or pack up and move.

I needed to start looking inside for answers, not outside. My internal dialogue needed to undergo a radical overhaul. I needed to own up to the fact that my life was in the state it was in because I had created it. I needed to take control of my life.

It was time to face the fact that no one was coming to save me. If I wanted a better future, I had to save myself.

*"Someday, somebody will walk into your life
and make you realize why it never worked out
with anyone else."*

-Unknown

CHAPTER IV:

Meeting Josh

It was through a series of small, seemingly unimportant events that led to the biggest and most important moment in my life—meeting my husband and business partner, Josh Zwagil.

At the time, Josh was the #1 Income Earner in a fuel additive network marketing company and co-owner of a marketing systems company on the side. At this point in my network marketing career, I had built a following on social media of nearly all network marketers. After years of trial and error, I realized the best way to grow a following was through target marketing. I began only connecting with other network marketers and people who possessed, in some way, the entrepreneurial spirit. It was easier to sell a person on an opportunity if they were open to it.

My experience with non-business minded people was not often successful. It was somewhat like chasing chickens, hoping one day they would turn into eagles and fly. They never would, or could, and at the end of it all, I was left with chicken shit all over me with not one of them flying to save their life.

Even with a following, I was still far from success, so I decided I'd just sell tools—marketing systems, lead capture pages, email autoresponders, etc. Without much thought or even realizing it, I started promoting Josh's system. I found his company through a mutual friend. Everything was going well until it was time for commissions to be paid. This "friend" kept the money and ran off. So, I did what anyone would do, I stopped promoting the company and told everyone to cancel. That got Josh's attention.

Josh wanted to meet whoever it was that made all those sales, then completely ransacked the business. To be fair, Josh didn't know he didn't pay me. He paid our friend on my behalf not knowing I was the one behind all the sales. So, he reached out to me on Facebook and was surprised to find out we were both in Baltimore. I was just getting out of the military and ended up living there after my son's father relocated there for work.

Josh asked me to meet him for coffee to hash out the money issue (and to also try to recruit me). He was a networker after all. I agreed to meet him.

Just as I was pulling up to the Starbucks, he called me and said he didn't drink coffee and that he'd rather meet for dinner instead. Real smooth. Chess moves already.

Things Are About to Change, Forever

We decided to meet at the Ale House in Columbia, about 20 miles from Baltimore. I got there anxiously early and found Josh circling the parking lot looking for a spot to park. Finally, he walks in. My heart dropped to my stomach. I was unusually nervous about meeting him because I think deep down I knew he was "the one." Meeting Mr. Right wouldn't have been a problem normally, but I was engaged to be married to someone else. Sidenote: My grandmother was married five times. When

I asked her if she'd ever thought about just being single for a while or being alone, she told me, "No, not really," with a sarcastic smile on her face. I guess you can say I was the same way.

For the record, I didn't seek out relationships, they just kind of gravitated toward me. So yes, I was engaged. To the wrong person. I immediately thought, "Crap, my whole life is about to change."

I didn't know where things would go with Josh but meeting him confirmed I needed to break off my engagement, stat. Even if things didn't work out with Josh and me, the spark I felt meant true love existed out there somewhere and it wasn't with my fiancé.

My next instinct was to sabotage any chance of Josh falling for me. I suppose I wanted to make sure he really wanted me, the real me—flaws, baggage, and all. I know this was extremely presumptuous of me on a first "business date" but I had a feeling we'd be together. At this point in my life I was too tired to put up a front to impress a guy. Been there, done that. It doesn't end well. So, I sat down and immediately began telling him all the negative things about myself. I told him I'd been divorced twice, had two children, was recently diagnosed with bipolar disorder, and was completely non-supportive of network marketing; the industry I knew he was passionate about and successful in.

In retrospect, I guess I was trying to tell him, "Stay away, if you know what's good for you." As much as I was attracted to him, I still wanted what was best for him, and at the time, I didn't feel that was me. I knew I had to do major work on myself to be worthy of a guy like him, so giving him a warning sign was my way of saying I was under construction and will be open later once I'm complete.

Somewhere during the conversation, the topic of network marketing came up. I said, "I'm done with network marketing. I'm leaving the industry."

Josh said, "It's funny you should say that because I'm going to launch my own network marketing company."

I said, "Well, have fun with that. I'll be rooting for you."

"No, you should join me," Josh said.

I shook my head. "No thanks, I'm out."

Behind the Curtain

The truth was, a decade of bad experiences with a parade of other network marketing companies had me feeling burned out and discouraged. I no longer thought it was possible for the average person to succeed—I'd seen behind the curtain and felt like the system was rigged.

Once, with a previous company, I was at their convention and one of the top reps approached me. "I like your style, and how edgy you are," the rep said. "We don't have a girl like you yet at the top—let's make a deal. We can give you a rank. We just have to move some people under your position."

My jaw dropped.

So, this is how it's done. Did I just get offered a higher rank in the company because I was a part of a demographic they were looking for? Seriously?

I'd heard rumors about stuff like this, people being offered positions without having earned their way there, but it seemed impossible that things like that actually happened. My heart sank thinking about it. I wanted to believe in network marketing.

Some people might have jumped at the chance, but I was disappointed. I wanted to believe there was a way to succeed in this industry without knowing people at the top. I wanted to know there was a way for the average person to succeed, starting out with nothing. If I didn't get this opportunity, could I have succeeded on my own? I needed to know it was possible so that I could go on stage and show people how it's possible for them, too.

I turned the offer down on the spot. The day after that, I left the company. I wanted to succeed honestly. I didn't want special favors or treatment. I didn't want top positions or fake volume under my organization. I wanted to go *through* the whole experience so that I could one day teach other people how I did it. Without the experience, I'd be nothing more than a spokesperson, and my future would still not be secure.

Rule:
Follow the leader.

Reality:
Follow the documented leader, but go your own way if what they're doing is wrong.

I told Josh about my previous experiences in network marketing and how little belief I had for the industry. I saw deals being made, I saw how people really got to the top, and I was heartbroken by it all. Network marketing was supposed to be my way out. It was supposed to bring hope and promise for a better life. I wanted the success stories to be real, but I wasn't sure if they could be.

He didn't fight me, and he didn't tell me I was wrong. He just listened and said, "I understand, Jenn, but give it one more shot, okay? Don't quit the industry. I've had success and I know how to build relationships and grow a business the right way. Just give it one more shot."

You'd Have to Do It Differently

I told Josh that if there was any chance of me changing my mind and joining his new company, he'd have to do it differently.

"Differently how?" he asked.

"Well, for starters, you'd have to have awesome products," I said. "I mean stuff that actually works and does what it's supposed to do." I wanted to sell products I could be proud of. Not ones that required lots of sales skills to push on people who would never otherwise buy them.

Josh smiled and waited for me to continue.

"And the compensation plan needs to be fair and not have any *gotchas*."

I was with more than one company that had breakage in their compensation plan, which meant, as soon as you hit a certain rank, your organization breaks off and no longer counts towards advancing further. You'd have to start over again with a new team.

Multi-level marketing, to my knowledge, was a leaky-bucket business. No matter how many times you plug the hole, a new one opens up and you start to sink again. I wanted there to be an easier way to get paid. I didn't want to need a degree to understand how to get paid, either.

"In one company I had to literally print out charts to try and figure out which leader I'd put where and if they quit I'd have to do it all over again. How does the average person succeed in a deal like that?" I said.

"Okay, go on," Josh said, with a smile as if he'd already thought of these things.

"No deal-making. Everyone starts from the bottom and works their way up. This is the only way to prove the opportunity is good on its own."

Josh said, "Okay, what else?"

"The company would have to have great customer service and support to the affiliates," I said. "Oh, and there'd have to be a really great system. MLM companies never provide a system, which is why so many reps end up building their own."

"That it?" Josh asked.

I thought for a long moment then said, "Yeah, that's it. I'm just saying it would have to be different from other companies."

Josh said, "That's why I'm starting my own company instead of joining one, Jenn. What if I promised to do things differently? Would you join?"

I said, "Well, if you're really going to do all that, then sure, I'll join you."

The Whole Thing Seemed Crazy

I found myself wondering if I was crazy, changing my whole life plan to follow this 23-year-old guy who was about to launch a network marketing company.

I was only five years older than him but felt lifetimes older. I had experienced so much before I had met him. At 28 years old I had been married not once but twice, had two kids, lived all over the country and had every job under the sun.

Josh had never been married and had no kids. What does he know about life? He had only been in one company, what could he possibly know? Why should I follow him?

I had no good answers, just a gut feeling. I felt I could trust him. And though I didn't know where things might go on a personal level—if we'd end up being a couple or if it would just be business—somehow I knew from the moment I saw him that he was the one I was destined to be with—like, *bam*, he's the one.

Even if I was wrong, the fact that I was considering it meant I had to go home and unravel my life by ending the engagement to my fiancé. So that's what I did.

I knew Josh wanted me to join his new company, but did that mean he wanted to be with *me*? And why would he? I was a train wreck at that point in my life. I'd told him everything. My cards were on the table.

Respectfully, Josh picked up the check. Then he said, "So, when can I see you again?" I laughed to myself wondering how on Earth everything I just said led him to wanting to see me again. I guess he was attracted to crazy.

It was about a week later, on our second date which happened to be at a casino, that we both figured out that we wanted to spend all our time together.

When people ask me how long it was before Josh and I knew we were in love with each other, I tell them it was somewhere between the main course and dessert. But joking aside, it was extremely fast, even if neither of us would admit it.

We were both afraid of love, but we both knew. We knew we were going to be together forever, even if neither of us had the courage to say it yet.

"Many of life's failures are people who did not know how close they were to success when they gave up."

-Thomas Edison

CHAPTER V:

Learning Not to Quit

Much of my time was spent traveling with Josh, chasing my kids and trying to figure out how to be successful in network marketing. Honestly, I have no idea how Josh and I stayed together—we were like two tornadoes, spinning in opposite directions, trying to figure out how to grow the business and not butt heads in our personal relationship. We were both so strong-willed and stubborn and had a lot to learn.

I was also focused on personal development, trying to become a better human—for him, and for me. I studied people like Jim Rohn, Bob Proctor, Esther and Jerry Hicks, and watched, "The Secret" to stay focused. It's no easy task to train yourself to think completely differently than you have for your entire life. I would get hopeful and positive, but then I'd get negative and doubtful again.

Going through this hard, painful process to become a success was more about who I was becoming in the process than the end result. Success is a process, a process I had to go through. No one could do it for me. Not Josh. Not friends or family. I had to go through it. Not around it. Not over it. Not under it. *Through* it.

I spent the majority of my life looking for a work-around, an alternative path, a short-cut—*a "hack"*—when all I had to do was go *through*.

The key for me was to learn acceptance. I had to accept where I was, right *now*. I had to stop living in the past and in the future. This was where I was now, and whatever life was trying to teach me, I had better learn to start listening.

A History of Quitting

It always seemed like everyone else knew what they wanted to do and had it all figured out. I had no idea what I wanted to do but had a list a mile long of what I knew I didn't want to do. I never felt like I belonged anywhere.

Rule:
Everyone has their limits, their breaking point.

Reality:
Limits are in the mind and we can push beyond them.

At one time or another, I went to community college, nursing school, and medical assistant school. I also studied to be a graphic designer and a hair stylist— I didn't finish any of them.

I held jobs in cable TV sales, phone sales, insurance sales, door-to-door sales, and car sales—and although I was good in these roles, I wasn't passionate about any of these jobs.

Pretty much everything you can imagine, I tried it, I hated it after two weeks, and in the rare instances where I didn't quit, I was fired. The only things I ever started and finished was my 4-year enlistment in the Army and getting my bachelor's degree in sales and marketing.

I dropped out of community college after getting a D in public speaking and a C- in communications. I didn't want those grades on my report card so quitting before they became final was an easier choice than having to retake them. It goes to show you that doing poor in a college class doesn't mean you'll do poor in real life and vice-versa.

After quitting these classes, I realized I was going to have to start paying back my student loans. Not having the money, I went back and took one class at a time. If you keep on going to school, you can keep deferring your loans. Genius. It took me eight years to get a four-year degree, but I graduated, and—thanks to network marketing—I paid my loans off too.

Self-Discipline, Focus, and Commitment

Besides my experience in college, the Army was another "job" I didn't quit. Not just because I wasn't allowed to but because I knew, deep down, I was meant to conquer it, not run from it. The biggest take-away from my military experience was that I learned to push myself beyond what I thought was possible. There were times I wasn't sure I could keep going. The rucksack was heavy, my feet were shattered, and I was beyond exhausted from staying up all night, but I learned to keep pushing even in moments I doubted myself.

What I learned in the Army wasn't self-discipline—it was *external* discipline. Someone standing over you, shouting orders and telling you to give them 20 push-ups was forced discipline coming from an *external source*, not from within.

Like most kids, I was disciplined by my parents when I did something wrong, and that's how I came to understand the word. Discipline meant punishment.

And since punishment was a bad thing, so was discipline.

Looking back, I don't recall my parents ever using the word in any other context—it was always used in connection to punishment.

Rule:
Having a lot of jobs means you're a flake. You should choose ONE career and stick with it.

I certainly was never taught that discipline was a good thing, or that I'd have to develop it someday if I wanted to be successful.

Reality:
Discovering what you don't want to do in life is just as helpful as figuring out what you do want to do. Don't be afraid to try new things.

I am not saying my parents are to blame for my lack of self-discipline—that's why it's called *self*-discipline. It was my responsibility to develop *self*-discipline and to motivate myself if I wanted to be successful.

Other people cannot make you self-disciplined. You must do it yourself. There is a saying in network marketing that goes, "If you want to become successful, you must master the mundane." Being disciplined enough to succeed requires that you decide to be disciplined, and show up every day, even on the uneventful days, the hard days, and the days you want to quit. Every action starts with a decision. I chose to become disciplined.

I wasn't always a person of high integrity, mostly because I grew up with the guidance from my church. I learned that if I messed up, all I had to do was ask for forgiveness from Jesus. This was a surefire way to avoid responsibility and taking the blame myself. It wasn't until later on in life that I realized being a good human was ultimately on me, and it was a decision like anything else. I became a person of integrity when I decided I was tired of asking for forgiveness. Doing the right thing from the start was much easier on my conscience and better for my relationships, too.

Deciding Not to Quit

Every new career was a disappointment, and whenever I encountered adversity, I gave up. I was willing to work *to* the point of adversity, but never *through* it. Before joining MyDailyChoice, I'd been in five or six different MLMs. I tried them all. *Tried.* I *tried* them, but I never really made the decision to *do* them.

Every time I joined a network marketing company, and it didn't work out, I thought, "Yep, I knew it, there's something wrong with this one, too." Sometimes it was the compensation plan, other times it was leadership or the product. Some of the companies had shady practices and less than excellent products, and I blamed these for my failure. But it never crossed my mind that the common dominator of all the opportunities I failed at was me. I simply never committed, I never wanted it bad enough; I suppose I didn't need it bad enough.

It wasn't until I joined MyDailyChoice that I decided to do the business—I mean *really* do it. In my mind, I didn't have a choice but to stay—leaving the business would also mean leaving Josh. He wasn't a quitter, and as long as he was committed to building this business, I had to stay and build it too. There were a lot of things I was still unsure of at this point in my life, but Josh wasn't one of them. He was probably the only thing I was sure of, the only constant in my universe.

I wanted to see what would happen if I didn't quit. Success is a slow process (or so I thought) under the best of circumstances. Quitting wasn't going to speed it up. The thought of returning to my old life, my old career, and my old struggles was motivation enough to keep moving forward, even when it felt like I wasn't going anywhere.

There are a lot of things most of us should quit doing. The one thing we should never quit on, however, is our dream. You may discover a thousand ways something doesn't work, but that just means you're closer to figuring out what does. Failure is progress if you keep going. It means you're getting closer with each lesson learned.

People are going to leave your team. They are going to quit their dreams and themselves. People are going to betray you along the way, and you will learn who your real friends are.

Your network will become bigger, but your circle will become smaller.

This is all part of the game. Don't take it personally. Network marketing is full of people who have tried it out in the "real world" and are looking for something else entirely. There are masses of people like you, waiting to break free of their shackles. You cannot become free if you give up and turn back to slavery. The only way to freedom is through conquering every challenge and trial along the way.

You will be pushed, you will be pulled, you will be stretched, you will be forcefully yanked out of your comfort zone. You will be ridiculed, you will be laughed at, you will be TESTED.

Network marketing isn't for the person who allows another's skepticism to keep them from their dreams. It's for the people who don't care what anyone thinks and is going to become successful one way or the other. You have to know deep in your bones you can do this, you can make it, you can reach the finish line, you can quit your job, you can move out of your current environment and reach into this alternative reality. It's a shift. First within our consciousness, and then in our physical reality. There is no way to cheat getting there—you have to do the work. You have to stay in the game to beat it.

Rule:
Never quit.

Reality:
Quit the things that insult your soul but not what brings you closer to your goals.

Fear of Success vs. Fear of Failure

Most people are afraid of failing. I became so used to failing it didn't faze me anymore. Looking back, I can see my biggest problem wasn't a fear of failure, it was a fear of success.

I believe the fear of success is just as great as the fear of failure for many people. People fear failure because they are afraid of criticism from others. This is one of the six basic fears according to Napoleon Hill's classic, "Think and Grow Rich." They are terrified to look like a fool if it doesn't work out, so they choose not to go after their higher goals and bigger dreams. Saving face from ridicule is more important than pursuing their dreams.

The risk just isn't worth it. They can't look stupid if they never try. But they also never live up to their full potential. They settle.

Some people convince themselves they've tried, when in reality they've only partially tried until met with (character building) resistance. Then they quit and create an excuse, thereby validating that success was never in it for them. It's a self-fulfilling prophecy.

I'll be honest, I loved the challenge of accomplishing a goal more than I ever feared looking stupid. I succeeded at virtually every job I had ever held despite the fact I hated being there. By nature, I'm a very competitive and ambitious person and this trumped any fear of looking lesser to people too afraid to even try. I might not have been a wild success yet, but I was leaps ahead of those too afraid to even give it a shot.

The fear of success, though, is rooted deep within the psyche of self-worth. People who are afraid of success *believe* they cannot get it, that they are not worthy.

Because of this, people subconsciously block their own success. How does a person come to *believe* these things about themselves? Through reinforced experiences and what we tell ourselves to be true. Much like the inner voice in our head, our experiences create the basis for who we will become. I had self-worth issues because I didn't feel loved or wanted by my father. I spent a lifetime trying to gain his approval and respect though always coming up short. If my own dad felt I wasn't worth having around in his life, then maybe I wasn't worth anything good that could happen to me, like success or long-lasting happiness.

But that wasn't to be my fate. Instead, I decided to be my own father in my life. I scooped myself up from my own self-pity and chose to love the little girl in me who desperately needed to be loved. If he couldn't love me, I would. And you know what? His opinions of me were simply that, his opinions, and I chose to allow myself the permission to override his opinion with my own. This was a conscious effort.

I decided from there that I was pretty awesome, actually. I was smart, I was funny, I was extremely good looking, (and humble, too). It was about time I decided to speak up for myself, to myself. I deserved love, happiness and all the success life could bring.

At some point on this journey, we have to choose to become everything we're missing from other people in our life. This and only this, makes us whole and prepared to succeed.

Fear Is a Head Game

The good news is fear doesn't exist anywhere outside our minds. I went through this with my son, Troy.

We have this rule in our family where, when you reach 10 years old, you're allowed to jump off the balcony into the pool. (Relax, it's engineered to be completely safe. There's a gate on our balcony that leads to the jumping area.)

Then Troy's moment finally arrived. He turned 10. For an entire year, he had waited for this opportunity. He stood up there, at the top of the balcony, deep in his own thoughts, for what seemed like an hour.

Time to intervene.

First, I tell him, "You can do it, Troy, just jump! Don't even think about it." He doesn't budge. So, I decide to try some reverse-psychology, or fear of loss. I say, "Alright, you don't have to do it. Get down, it's okay to give up." He's still thinking. For extra measure I add on: "You're going to have to live with the regret of never experiencing this, but don't worry. Maybe it's not for you."

My coaching isn't working. He's still standing there, looking down at the water. I decide that, rather than telling him what to do, to ask a question. "What's stopping you from jumping, Troy?"

Rule:
Put your best foot forward.

He launches in a series of *what ifs*. What if I get hurt? What if something happens? What if... what if... what if...?

Reality:
Put any foot forward. Just start. Just jump!

I said, "Would you be thinking about all that stuff if the building behind you was on fire?"

He says, "No, I would just jump."

"So now all you have to do is eliminate the fear that's in your mind, because that's the only place it exists," I said. "If the building behind you *was* on fire, you would jump into the pool with no problem, but because it's *not* on fire, you can't jump?"

I can see him thinking.

In one reality, he doesn't jump and with that he is left with the false feeling of safety, but also regret. In another reality he jumps, he risks not making it successfully, but is rewarded with the exhilarating experience of living life in the flow of your own creation.

He decides. Seconds later, he jumps. He's conquered his fear.

Everything Is a Process

Overcoming fear is a process. Success is a process. Happiness is a process. Confidence and courage are processes, too. None of them are things you can buy or find lying on the ground by the curb. They have to be worked through.

It was hard to come to grips with the fact that I'd spent so much of my life in a state of unconscious, wishful thinking. It's an okay place to start, but it's not a good place to stay. Wishing must eventually give way to doing. Doing the things necessary to create change. Here I was, with a dream of someday changing the world, and I hadn't even taken the time to change myself.

It didn't take Josh long to identify my main problem, and it wasn't my bank account. It was my mindset. Josh said, "You are super negative. You've got a 'broke' mindset."

"I'm not negative," I said defensively. "I'm just telling the truth. I'm realistic. These are things I am actually experiencing."

Rule:
Money is money.

Reality:
Money is energy.

When Josh and I were first dating, we lived in the same apartment building but in separate apartments. Each day we'd walk down to get our mail together. I would open my mailbox and see an assortment of bills. Then Josh would open his mailbox, and there would be checks.

Mailbox money.

"I don't understand it, Josh. Your mailbox always has money coming in, and mine always has money going out."

He said, "I expect there to be checks, so there are checks."

It made me crazy, thinking about how he could just attract money like that. He understood that money is energy, just like everything else, which is why he was a money magnet, and why I repelled it.

The idea that we live in a thought universe, and that we can produce tangible riches from formless substance, hadn't hit me yet.

But the proof was in Josh's mailbox. Whatever he was doing was working. What I was doing wasn't.

Josh said, "Listen, I've had success in this industry. I know how it works. I can teach you if you want."

For all my weaknesses at the time, at least I was coachable. I said, "Great, teach me, I am ready to learn."

"Everything is energy, that's all there is to it. Match the frequency of the reality you want, and you cannot help but get that reality. It cannot be any other way."

-Albert Einstein

CHAPTER VI:
Energy, Frequency & Vibration

Nikola Tesla, one of the most brilliant humans to ever walk the planet, understood the big picture of how the universe worked before most everyone else when he said:

"If you want to find the secrets of the universe, think in terms of energy, frequency and vibration."

Everything is made of energy and has its own unique vibration: humans, animals, plants, light, sounds, and even thoughts.

The air around us is filled with hundreds of radio waves, one for every radio station on the dial, each operating at a different frequency. Without a radio receiver, you can't hear them. Just because we can't hear them, doesn't mean they're not there. In fact, humans are electromagnetic beings. Even our heartbeat beats to its own electromagnetic frequency.

On the electromagnetic spectrum, humans can only perceive 1-4% through visible light. The other 96-99% is virtually undetected to the human eye. This means, there is a lot going on around us we do not see.

VISIBLE SPECTRUM

VISIBLE LIGHT

GAMMA RAYS	X-RAYS	UV	INFRARED	RADIO WAVES		
				RADAR	TV FM	AM
0,0001 nm	0,01 nm	10 nm	1000 nm	0,01 cm	1 cm	1 m	100 m

| 400 nm | 500 nm | 600 nm | 700 nm |

There's a famous philosophical question that goes, *if a tree falls in the woods and no one is there to hear it, does it make a noise?* There is quite a debate around this.

In my opinion, it doesn't. Sound requires a receiver, an eardrum for the vibration to reach. If no one is there to hear the sound, there's vibration, but there is no sound. If the receiver is off by just a fraction, all you get is static.

What Frequencies Are We Tuned To?

It's not only radio waves. *Everything has its own frequency.* One of the most significant turning points in my success journey came from learning this.

Success vibrates at a frequency. Happiness vibrates at a frequency. Wealth vibrates at a frequency. So does failure, hate, and poverty. They all operate at their own frequency. It's no coincidence that Bob Marley, the famous Rastafarian musician, tuned his music to 432 Hz, which is believed to coincide with DNA synthesis, which closely resemble the frequency of the Earth, the Schumann Resonance. In theory, his music raised the vibration of all who listened as well as the vibration of the Earth itself. Alternatively, music today is broadcasted over 440 Hz, which is said to cause disharmony, stress and negative emotions among humans.

I decided that if I wanted to attract abundance into my life, I needed to become finely tuned to the frequency of abundance. If I wanted to achieve massive success, I needed to operate at the frequency of success and change my energy to match that frequency. It wasn't the universe's job to change the way it operated. *It was mine.*

Of course, I don't take credit for coming up with any of these concepts. I *do* take credit for seeking them out, learning them, and taking action.

I remember constantly being in situations where my every thought was, "How am I going to be able to pay my bills this month?" This is survival thinking, not possibility thinking.

I also believed the rule that said you needed money to make money. It seemed crazy that money could be manifested with nothing more than the power of thought. The idea that "thought was currency" was foreign to me.

What I know now is, like everything else in the universe, money *is* energy. As long as I was in the flow of receiving money and tuned into the right frequency, I could surely attract it.

Functionally Broke

Most people think of being broke as not having a penny to your name. That's not the kind of broke I was, although, I have been penniless at times, too. I'm talking about being *functionally broke.*

I had barely enough money pay the bills. And if it was a good month, I had a little extra.

Rule:
It takes money to make money.

Because I was predominately in sales jobs, my income fluctuated. Some months were great and other months I was one disaster away from an economic meltdown.

Reality:
It takes being on the same frequency as money, to make money.

No one plans on being broke. I sure didn't. I kept thinking I was on the path to becoming wealthy. Sure, the path had changed multiple times and there were certainly roadblocks and forks in the road, but it was always my intent to pursue success to the finish line. Yet, year after year, I found myself no closer to the life I dreamed of having.

Being broke isn't just a state of income, it's a state of mind. If you *think* you're broke and you *feel* broke, it doesn't matter how much money you have in the bank—*you're broke.*

More than I wanted money, I wanted time. I wanted to have enough money to not have to think about money. The people who have the least money think about it the most. And the people who have tons of money think of it very little. I wanted to be so rich I didn't have to think about it anymore. I wanted just to live limitlessly.

Being functionally broke means not having time freedom.

You still have to work for money. As long as you work for money, you remain owned by it.

Playing small keeps you broke. Staying safe keeps your broke. Hanging around broke friends keeps you broke. Listening to broke opinions keeps you broke. Not taking action keeps you broke.

To *shift* into the consciousness and vibration of wealth and abundance, you must:

Play it big. Do not fear life.

Step outside of your comfort zone regularly.

Surround yourself by positive, wealth-conscious people.

Listen to thought leaders who have what you want.

Take action immediately.

Words Are Magic Spells

Your vocabulary and everything that you feel about the words you are saying on a regular basis serve as the foundation of what you are creating in the real world.

If you're talking about your problems, then you are on a repeat cycle of creating problems. And the opposite is true, as well. If your language is around positive aspects, then you are on a repeat cycle of creating positive results. In other words, *your words are your magic spells.* Of course, it's more than just speaking words. You must mean them. You must feel them. You must become them. Words that are amplified by emotion will manifest through action.

Rule:
Speaking positively will create a positive life.

Everything is vibrating. The words on this page. The thoughts in our mind. What we say. Everything. If we are on the wrong frequency from what we say we want, it will never manifest. It's a mismatch.

Reality:
Speaking positively and meaning it will create a positive life.

We're on the wrong frequency. *The universe always delivers to us that which we are vibrating.*

When people tell themselves the same old story, over and over again, they're literally on a subconscious loop. If you're emotionally invested in your old story, then that is what you're going to be creating over and over again. You will never create anything different.

Thoughts Are Unspoken Words

Where do words come from? Thoughts, of course, from our mind. The words that come out of our mouths always start as thoughts, and only then do they come out as words—words that will set in motion the frequency of where we're going to end up. Because of this I have become very, very, aware of saying anything I don't want to create.

Even when words aren't said but only *thought*, the thought itself can manifest into physical reality if enough emotion is behind it and action is taken. What is being thought about is being created whether we like it or not. The universe has no biases. It doesn't care if you want to see greatness or failure, problems or opportunities, happiness or sadness—whether your words and thoughts are for good or evil, negative or positive—it doesn't make any difference. We live on a planet of duality: good and evil; positive and negative. Everything is in perfect balance and harmony within its ecosystem. The universe doesn't know the difference between the two, only we perceive that. We must be mindful of what we are internalizing because what we accept as real in the mind will surely become our reality.

Rule:
The past cannot be changed.

Reality:
How we feel about the past can be changed, and that is where we find peace.

Whatever you're focusing on gives it power to manifest. Our *awareness* is our power.

We create what we think about.

The Past Can't Be Changed

Success is, in large part, determined by the stories we tell ourselves and others. I was never going to have the *future* I wanted if my mental energy and focus were spent thinking about the *past*.

Early on in my network marketing career, most of my focus was on my past—where I came *from*, what was *behind* me. It's hard to visualize a different future when I was subconsciously using my energy to mentally repeat life events.

I realized that if I was going to become who I was meant to be, I needed to make peace with my past. We can't change the things in our lives that happened to us, but we can change how we feel about the things that happened to us. As much as I'd like to say there's a magic wand to erase all the things I had been through, I realized what I had been through is exactly what prepared me for the life I have now.

Instead of being a victim in my story, I chose to become the hero. I had to accept the fact that every challenge, every heartbreak, every betrayal, and every letdown, were experiences I needed to be molded into the person I am today.

Rewriting My Story

Like many people who are serious about personal development, I had been into journaling. I'd kept journals for years and had stacks of them. Then, one year, I got angry about where life had taken me and burned them in a charcoal grill in the backyard. I thought that if I burned my journals, I'd extinguish my past. Which didn't work. The past only exists in our mind, nowhere else. Burning the journals was a creative attempt to deal with my pain but it didn't bring the peace I had hoped.

Letting go of my past wasn't the answer. *I needed to need to re-write my story.*

The story of my past I had been telling kept me tethered to it. So, I flipped the script. Instead of a period at the end of that story, I put a comma and kept writing. My past became a chapter in my book full of wisdom and lessons learned, instead of an excuse for self-pity.

My solution to the problem was to stop trying to forget about my past and to start thinking about it differently. I took all my stories and I transformed them into something different, with positive meanings rather than negative meanings. The past could not be changed, but how I interpreted it could.

Rule:
The universe is random.

Reality:
The universe is conscious.

Changing the Meaning of Past Events

Albert Einstein said, "The most important decision we make is whether we believe in a friendly or hostile universe." Because of my upbringing, I always felt like I lived in a hostile universe. In a hostile universe, things happen to you, not for you. I always felt the universe had it in for me. It was not looking out for me.

No wonder good things weren't happening to me. I was treating the world like it was my enemy. I needed friends, not enemies. And I loved Josh too much to let our relationship end the way my past relationships had. If I wanted a happy ending, I needed to rewrite the meaning of my past.

First, I decided that the universe was here to help me, not hurt me, and that everything in my past had happened *for* me, not *to* me. Those failed relationships didn't happen to destroy me, they happened to make me stronger and wiser.

The same was true for my business failures. They all made me better, not worse. Pain taught me strength. Abandonment taught me love. Everything I've ever experienced has given me building blocks of knowledge that I can pass on to others. For that reason, I'm grateful for my story, even as painful as it was to live through.

My journey led me through trials that showed me how I could not only survive but become anyone I wanted to become with a shift in consciousness.

It was this type of thinking that allowed me to feel I was worthy to be Josh's equal. He may have had success in his past, but I could have success in our future.

*"The most difficult thing is the decision to act.
The rest is merely tenacity."*

-Amelia Earhart

CHAPTER VII:

MyDailyChoice

J osh had a vision of building a company that would offer multiple product brands under one roof. He had witnessed some of the greatest companies lose their way from pigeon-holing themselves to one idea or product line and then not being able to pivot successfully to another when wanting to launch something new.

From a consumer standpoint, MyDailyChoice would offer products people could easily identify with and, as the name suggests, would be used daily. From the opportunity side, he wanted to give people the choice as to how they wanted to build their business, whether they wanted to build it online or offline, and how they wanted to spend their rewards in the compensation plan.

He believed there were several key components that made for a great network marketing company, which he called, the four pillars. He put them together so that the average person who got involved, either part-time or full-time, had a real chance to succeed. It was everything Josh and I had agreed on in our first conversation.

The First Pillar is the House of Brands.

MyDailyChoice is the parent company to multiple brand offerings such as Daily Sprays, HempWorx, Mantra, High Life Travel, Akashx, and so on. This is truly unique in the network marketing industry.

Whether you want to sell CBD oil, essential oils, travel services, nutritional products, or education on Forex and Cryptocurrencies, there is literally a brand for everyone. We saw a trend early on of people leaving companies to promote new products, so we decided to be a company that offers many products to help keep the affiliate's business booming.

We are so confident in the performance of our products we offer a 60-day money back guarantee. All our products are designed to improve a person's wellness and overall lifestyle. Our website, www.mydailychoice.com, is truly a unique, one-stop shopping experience for the new customer or affiliate.

The Second Pillar is the Compensation Plan.

MyDailyChoice pays up to 85% of the business volume the affiliate generates, whereas the industry standard is half that. Our compensation plan is a hybrid binary-unilevel. Usually, a compensation plan is either a binary or unilevel.

Each compensation structure has its pros and cons. A binary creates teamwork and builds faster but has a cap on how much can be earned. A unilevel has a higher earning potential but doesn't duplicate as fast. Personally, I would run away from a binary or a unilevel.

A hybrid binary-unilevel brings the best of both worlds together. It allows affiliates to recruit personally, build a large team, and offer support to everyone within their organization.

There are 8 different categories in which to get paid and we have pretty much every payout option you can imagine (even precious metals and cryptocurrency.)

And because the compensation plan is non-restrictive, it's easier to hit ranks. In my experience, it was nearly impossible to hit the middle ranks let alone the top ranks. In MyDailyChoice it's simply based on the volume your organization is bringing in. There are minimal qualifiers to get paid out on which gives the newest person a real shot to earn an income.

The Third Pillar is The Free Marketing System.

The Free Marketing System consists of lead capture pages, auto responders, weekly follow up emails, a contact manager, and a mobile app to manage content and prospects. The system is designed to get the prospect to take action through what we call, "the Success Line."

Every Thursday night at midnight, we have a cut off. The cut off is to reward action takers. If you take action now and upgrade to an affiliate you will earn off the volume generated by those who come in after you. If you don't take action now, those who upgrade before you will earn off your volume generated should you choose to become an affiliate later on. This creates urgency for the new person to get in, get started and build their team quickly.

Most companies do not have a marketing system in place. The ones that do, charge for it, leaving the affiliate to pay out of their own pocket. MyDailyChoice covers the cost at no expense to the affiliate.

The <u>Fourth</u> Pillar is Company Culture.

To us, this is everything. Josh and I were first affiliates before we became owners. We had real life experience in the field as leaders before we ever stepped foot into the corporate world. We understand the struggle affiliates face every day. We know what it's like to build a team and have them quit and be at the mercy of misguided company changes. We know how to build real relationships with real people, and this sets us apart from our competition. One thing we both experienced as affiliates in the field is corporate greed. Compensation plans would change, leaving the affiliate working for less pay for the same work. It has always been our mission to put the affiliate first. To become a legacy company people can call "home."

We offer exclusive training and mentorship for our affiliates and support their teams when they need it most. And because of our rapid, explosive success, we have surrounded ourselves with the best corporate staff money could buy.

Our philosophy is simple: Always be improving. We built this company from the bottom, with nothing, but continue to outperform ourselves.

Our goal is not to impress people, it's to provide real families with a way out of the grind, the 9-5, the work for 50 years and hope to retire path. We want to be the rescue team, the life raft, and the hope that helps people create the life of their dreams.

When I joined as an affiliate in 2014, stupidly in love with the CEO, I had no idea the man I was dating was master planning the world's biggest comeback in the network marketing industry. It was the first time the people vs. the investors, corporate bigwigs and the paid to play leadership were the ones in the driver's seat.

MyDailyChoice was the underdog and I was the wildcard that no one saw coming.

Building from the Bottom Up

Most network marketing companies, like most big companies, are built from the top down. They start with a business plan, raise gobs of money, hire a CEO who assembles an executive team, lease corporate offices, build a distribution warehouse, fill it with inventory, and train a customer service department to handle the day-to-day details. Then—after they have got all their ducks in a row—they go out and make deals with leaders who will grow teams and make sales.

That is how it's done.

Not us. MyDailyChoice was built from the bottom up.

One reason we did it this way was because we knew long-term success depended almost entirely on the strength of the leaders who would build our affiliate network. The other reason was because we were working on a shoestring budget. The little money we did have was used for our initial product inventory.

We went out and recruited affiliates first and built the infrastructure of the company after the fact. As the business grew, we found ourselves realizing we needed many departments to run things properly. We needed a customer service team, a whole warehouse crew, human resources, international expansion people, supply chain experts, operational management, and marketing, just to name a few.

We started out with just Josh, me and a couple others running the whole company. I would be lying if I said we had it all figured out from day one. We didn't. We learned everything as we went along and as we needed to learn it. To this day we are still improving. We are still growing and rising to the many challenges that come with running a hundred million dollar a year business.

I Had a Quick Start

We launched MyDailyChoice in November 2014 in a small apartment in Towson, Maryland, with a product line comprised of three nutritional sprays.

Amazingly, I hit 25K—the third rank in the company in my first month, finding myself at the top of the leaderboard and earning nearly $6,000 in commissions.

It was the first time in a long time that I had hope for the industry. The compensation plan paid more than anything I had ever experienced, and I thought maybe this was actually going to work.

Then, in my second month, I dropped to 10K. Worse still, my numbers didn't improve for several months. I quickly discovered that the universe has an interesting way of putting you back where you belong, especially if you reach success too fast. I was a 25K performer on paper, but I was still operating with a 5K mindset. I knew how to recruit but didn't know how to build a team, or how to keep people engaged month after month. My heart wanted success, but my mindset was filled with a lack of limiting beliefs.

Stay Focused, Jenna

"You have to learn to stay focused," Josh said.

"I am focused," I said.

"No, Jenn, you're not."

He was right.

I would often let myself get involved in a gazillion things, convincing myself that because I was busy, I was accomplishing something. Working hard was not enough, and Josh could see what I couldn't.

Eventually, he encouraged me to take a seriously bold move. "You need to quit your job," he said.

"Quit my job? I can't quit my job!" I said. "I'm a single mom with two kids."

Rule:
Success requires that you stay busy.

Reality:
Success requires that you stay focused.

"If this business is ever going to work, you have to trust me," Josh said. "And I'm not going to waste my time mentoring you if you're not going to be all-in."

I took a leap of faith and did what he asked. I quit my job.

Filing for Bankruptcy

I filed for bankruptcy four months after Josh talked me into quitting my job. And don't think I didn't hold it over him. I used it against him every chance I got. We fought like crazy over it. I would say things like, "Maybe you had success in the past, but what if it doesn't work now?"

How did he respond?

The way he always did. "Stay focused, Jenna. Just stay focused, it's going to happen. I went through the same thing you're going through."

And then he hit me with what I knew to be true but still didn't want to face. "And by the way, Jenna, the reason you're going bankrupt isn't because of me, it's because you're negative about the business. Deep down you want to believe this will work but you won't let yourself really believe it. You don't want to get your hopes up, so you're finding every excuse for why it won't work instead of focusing on how it can."

It was hard to hear, but he was right.

It wasn't enough to work in the business, or even on the business. More than anything, I needed to work on myself. And I needed to stay the course.

Rule:
Make a plan
and stick to it.

Reality:
Choose a direction
and stick to it. Plans
constantly change.

Learning to Commit

The most interesting thing about dating the CEO is not being able to quit very easily. If I were just an affiliate, I don't know that I would have stayed in the game during the tough times. Sounds harsh, but it's true. People think the opposite, of course. People think that if you've got a connection to the top it's somehow easier, but it wasn't. In many ways it was harder.

Because of our relationship, a lot of work I did went unnoticed. I'd hit the top of the leaderboard, and the prize would go to the second-place winner because he didn't want it to look like I was getting special treatment. I would hit a top rank and wouldn't get the same recognition.

One guy in our business would not join me until I showed him my back office. He assumed my success was because of Josh. I showed him the months and months of little to no pay. I showed him the struggle. I showed him the beginning of my success and where it came from. HempWorx—the brand I had created and that was responsible for 80% of company growth. It was truly a team effort. If it weren't for Josh, though, I might not have stayed the course long enough to see HempWorx come to life.

I was in a place in my life where failure had beaten me down to the point that it hurt to believe in anything. Josh didn't have a ton of bad experiences; he had a success story under his belt and knew the way even in the darkest of times. It was like hiking off trail, in the dark, in the middle of the woods, and you've got no cell phone reception and you've just run out of food and water. I wanted to set off the flares and wait for the rescue team, and Josh wanted to keep going because he knew at the end of the dark, scary part was paradise. I had to trust that. It's all I had left.

As imperfect as our business was in the beginning, I still believed in Josh. More than I believed in myself. I risked everything to follow this guy off into the wilderness but somehow knew it was the path I was meant to take. I knew it wouldn't be easy, but I also knew there was no other way to accomplish our goals but to stay the course. I was committed first to him, and second to the business. As a result, both our relationship and our company became a huge success despite every imaginable adversity.

Not a 'Get Rich Quick' Scheme

Network marketing offers many benefits, and I am sold on it as a viable way to earn an above average living. But getting rich quick isn't one of them. It takes time to learn how it works, climb through the ranks, and build a team. There's no guarantee you will succeed fast, but there is a guarantee that if you do the right things long enough, you will succeed eventually.

At its core, network marketing is a mental game—a game of knowing how to deal with rejection and the up and down roller coaster ride of being an entrepreneur. And those who think any of that is something that can be mastered quickly and easily isn't approaching this business realistically.

People ask me, "How did you do it, Jenna? How did you work your way to the top? What's the secret?" The answer is a long one, one that contains a lifetime of learning, which is the main reason I wrote this book. But if I had to identify a moment, a moment I went from someone who couldn't win to someone who could, I would say it's this:

Rule:
People need to work toward success.

Reality:
Before you start working toward success, you need to decide to succeed.

It was the moment I decided to succeed.

That was it.

The story of my life can be divided into two distinct halves: the first half is everything that happened *before* I made the decision to succeed, and the second half is everything *after* I decided to succeed. I made the decision to stop *trying* and get on with making it happen.

I Decided to Stop 'Trying'

Most people come into this business with the idea of *giving it a try, giving it a shot*. I know this is true because I was one of those people once.

I was always busy *trying* but never really *deciding*. Each time I tried a new opportunity and didn't make money in the first 30 days, I quit. How ridiculous.

Very few businesses make a profit in their first year let alone their first 30 days. Amazon didn't make a profit for seven years.

Successful professional network marketers do not *try*, they make a commitment to stick with it for as long as it takes. The length of time does not matter. They don't care if it takes three weeks, or three months, or three years—whatever it takes, they're committed and all-in. They don't say, *"I'm going to try this thing."* As Yoda from Star Wars famously said, "There is no try, there is only do."

Everyone wants success to be a 100-yard dash. But if you treat the business like a sprint, you are destined to fail. Success is never a sprint, it's always a marathon. And marathons require stamina and commitment, something I had never done until I joined MyDailyChoice.

Looking back now I see that I probably could have been successful with any one of the network marketing companies I'd joined. All I had to do was decide to be successful. If I had been committed and truly *decided* to succeed, I could have risen to the top in any one of them sooner.

"Progress is not achieved by luck or accident,
but by working on yourself daily."

-Epictetus

CHAPTER VIII:

Working on Myself

One of the most defining moments in my life came in 2016, on my 30th birthday. I was sitting in a bar, by myself, because I was reminded year after year for the past seven years that I didn't matter to my dad. I wasn't worth a phone call, a text, a card in the mail. The day I was born you would think would be a momentous occasion for him worth remembering, but he didn't. If he did remember, he didn't show it. Every year on my birthday since he'd been gone, I had tried to disappear from everyone, drawing as little attention to the day as possible because, honestly, it wasn't worth celebrating without the one person from whom I so desperately needed acknowledgement.

Every year I would wait to see if he would text me, and year after year of watching my phone, he never did. And every year, even though I vowed not to text him, I would always give in. "Hey, remember me?" I never got a response.

So, there I was on my 30th birthday, feeling as low as I can ever remember. Maybe it was from the vodka—a bit of "liquid courage" as they say—I'm not sure, but I found myself texting him, pouring my heart out, hoping he'd find it within himself to show an ounce of care for me. To my surprise, this time, he responded.

After seven years of no response, he'd just written me back.

His text was short: "For all your problems, talk to your other parents." My dad had just denied me as his daughter. Officially.

I remember feeling so worthless, so unloved. And in my mind, I said to myself, "What could I have possibly done to deserve this?" I had children myself, and there were no scenarios I could think of that would warrant this blatant abandonment. Could I abandon my own children the way he so carelessly put me on a shelf to easily forget about? No. I couldn't.

The irony of it all was that he had adopted three boys whose own father abandoned them, yet here I was, his own biological child that he took part in creating, tossed to the side like unwanted clothes that no longer fit. I no longer fit into his life, and he couldn't have made it clearer that I didn't matter.

I'm not telling you this to make you feel sorry for me. I'm telling you this to make the point that everybody has a story. Everybody.

Everybody has something in their past that damaged them, that's holding them back. I've never met anyone who hasn't had something tragic or painful happen to them. I don't know what your thing is, but I know you had something happen that you've been carrying for years, like a heavy set of unwanted baggage. Feeling unloved by my dad was *my* baggage. This was the thing that was stopping me from being happy, and ultimately, successful.

A Weight Had Been Lifted

I cried my eyes out that night. Something inside just...*broke*. I allowed all the shattered pieces of me to be just that. I took in all the pain, and deep down somewhere in the rubble and ash I found acceptance. The burden of this weight had suddenly been lifted from my heart. It was the first time I felt I could breathe. It was the first time I felt I didn't need his love or validation to be whole. I knew I had to stop searching for acceptance and love *out there* and to start loving myself, right now. Even if no one else loved me, and as imperfect as I was, *I* would love myself. I would be the parent I needed in my life. I could be whole without anyone else. I was whole the entire time. I *was* good enough. I *was* worthy. I deserved everything I set out to achieve and more. I owed it to myself to never let anyone make me think otherwise again.

Rule:
We cannot control our thoughts.

Reality:
Learning to control your thoughts is personal development.

A lot of us grow up with people telling us over and over that we're not good enough, that we can't do something, that our ideas and dreams are stupid or unrealistic. We're told these things so often that eventually we begin to believe them. Then we start repeating these things to ourselves, again and again. The question is, whose voice is it?

It's the subconscious soundtrack of our past experiences.

The good news is, we can change it. We are in control, no one else. I decided I was going to stop taking orders from the voice in my head and instead, give that voice some direction and guidance. While it may seem impossible to monitor our thoughts, we can tell if we are in alignment with our goals by how we *feel*. Our emotions tell us if we are on track or not. If we are super stressed and upset we are out of alignment. If we are joyful, happy and at peace, we are in alignment. Our thoughts are the starting point of all we manifest. Thoughts fueled by emotion backed by action cause creation. If we want to create the life of our dreams, we must pay attention to how we feel and the quality of our thoughts.

Forgiveness Over Anger

I will never forget the pain or the heartache I experienced as a child and as an adult learning to navigate the waters of "real life" alone. These experiences serve as a reminder to never look "out there" for love and acceptance again. Humans are imperfect, even the ones we think shouldn't be, such as our parents. When we are young, there's this hero complex we have for them where they can do no wrong.

I remember feeling like my dad was my hero. For no reason other than he was my dad. I even wrote a song about it because writing music was my therapy. Even though we feel like the people in our life who shouldn't do us wrong, do, it's still on us to forgive. Forgiveness is more about inner peace than anything else. It's learning to accept things as they are and being okay anyway.

I forgave my dad for everything. For his lack of care. For his lack of contact. For his thoughtlessness. I got to a place where I had to find peace. I would still love him and want him in my life should he choose to be, but I would probably always guard my heart and not allow it to break again. Though my heart had become calloused, I found strength and happiness in continuing to put love out into the world.

When I tell this story, some people say, "How could you forgive someone who hurt you so badly? I would never forgive them. Never, never, never."

Very simply, I realized he was just playing the role in my life that he *had* to play—a role that helped make me strong, made me independent, and made my success possible. I will never understand how or why he made the decisions he did, but maybe it's not for me to understand. Everyone deals with pain in their own way, with the tools they've been given. Maybe he was unconsciously repeating a generational curse passed down to him by his father, and his father's father.

I thought about this so many times, and what I know now is that had my father not been gone, had he not broken my heart, I wouldn't be who I am today. So now I thank him for it, I really do. He helped me realize nobody can ever control how I feel about myself ever again. From this point on, I would be the one to decide that. This gave me much peace and strength.

A full year later, I reached out to him again, but this time I changed my approach. Instead of reaching out in anger and hurt, I simply asked him to grab a cup of coffee with me.

To my complete shock, he agreed.

He, my stepmom, and Josh and I met up at the local coffee shop near their house when Josh and I were in town visiting friends. We talked about everything. They apologized, and I did too, for whatever reason they had for wanting to leave me. Things may never go back to how they were before, but we can choose to grow toward understanding and acceptance. We can choose to coexist in each other's lives peacefully and work toward a better relationship.

He wasn't a bad father. In fact, he was a really good one. I think that's why it hurt so much when he left. Had he never been there, I wouldn't have missed him. But I did.

He taught me how to take care of a home, animals, even how to patch holes in the wall and change my oil. Without his presence in my life growing up, I would've never had the work ethic I do today. I was more than equipped to live life when I left his home, which is the point of raising kids.

Things weren't perfect. They never are for anyone. But that's what makes living life interesting and for that I am humbled and grateful.

Throwing Myself into Self-Development

One of the rules I broke early on was not taking my parents' advice to go to a four-year college straight out of high school. They wanted me to take the traditional route and get a degree or at least find a stable, secure job I could stay at for several years. Why?

Because it was the path *they* took.

I made my living in network marketing, which is probably the last career a parent wishes for their kids to dedicate their life to. Many people in society believe MLM is synonymous with pyramid scheme. They say things like, "Only the people at the top make money." Or, "I just couldn't sell to my friends and family members." And, "I had a friend doing one of those things and that person was never successful."

They believe it's a scam.

The real scam is the American Dream of working a 9-5 and being able to comfortably retire. This may have existed a generation ago, but it doesn't exist today.

My parents on my dad's side have master's degrees. My parents on my mom's side have two-year and four-year degrees. By any measure, they would be thought of as smart. They both made decent money, especially after working in their careers for several years. They appeared to be successful and, by many measures, were.

But "successful" in America is making just enough to retire. It's hopefully having enough money to last until you die, which can be a difficult thing to plan for on a fixed income. Not to mention, the facts are in. People are having a really hard time retiring anymore.

According to a survey conducted by the Federal Reserve, over 30 percent of Americans reported having no retirement savings or pension.

I Tried Doing It Their Way

I tried to do it their way, I really did. But when I became an adult, I quickly realized I did not want to go down that path. I didn't want "just enough," I wanted more than enough, and I wanted to create generational wealth to be passed down to my children and grandchildren. The societal rule that getting a degree is critical to success and happiness is not always true.

I'm not denying that there are certain fields that require a formal education. You can't be a doctor or a lawyer or an astronaut or a math professor without one. But beyond that? Most formal education is a scam.

In school, you memorize facts, and then you're tested on it. Specifically, remembering names and dates and "facts" that have been selected for us to learn. And that is supposed to be an indicator of intelligence in our society.

Critical thinking is not being applied through the school system. They teach you what to think, not how to think. And if you question their beliefs, you're an outsider.

Rule:
Formal education is the guaranteed path to success.

The world does not need more people who are just getting by. It needs people who are brave enough to chase their dreams and live up to their full potential.

Reality:
Self-education is the only way to take control of your future.

Education vs. Being Educated

What I've discovered is that people who are serious about success are serious about educating themselves. As Jim Rohn said, "Formal education will make you a living; self-education will make you a fortune."

The information people need to be tremendously successful is not being taught in the classroom. It's in running towards your goals, failing fast, and reading books and studying those who have succeeded before you.

When I wanted to learn social media, I followed and studied top social media marketers. When I wanted to learn graphic design, I watched hundreds of hours of tutorials on YouTube. When I wanted to learn the concepts of the Law of Attraction and Vibration, I studied Napoleon Hill, Earl Nightingale and Bob

Proctor. Self-education is the act of educating yourself. It's learning the skills you need to level up in your life. It's embracing the continual process of becoming your best self.

Reading Changes You

People wonder why anyone would read the same book again and again. Because that's what it takes to get the most out of a book. Okay, but why read it again and again? It's the same book, it hasn't changed. No, it hasn't changed—but *you* have.

For example, I've read "Think and Grow Rich" by Napoleon Hill at least 20 times, and every time I learn something different. I pick up some little nugget of wisdom I missed before. Because every time I read the book, *I'm* different.

Rule:
Successful people read.

The me that reads "Think and Grow Rich" today is not the same me that read it last month or last year.

Reality:
Successful people don't just read, they study.

If you've ever watched a movie with a complicated plot for a second time, you know what I'm talking about. You see things you missed before. Small things an actor said, that didn't make sense the first time you watched it, do now.

No one who studies any subject with the intent of mastering it reads books only once. They read them multiple times. I've been telling people for years how important it is to read. I'd like to amend that. It's not just important to read, it's important to *study*. Because the goal is not to see how many books you can get through, it's to see how many can get through to you.

Leaders Are Readers

I had the privilege to meet and work with Bob Proctor over the last few years. When I met him, I asked him what he was currently reading. He said, in all his years, he'd never had anyone ask him that. I wondered what a guy like him could possibly be learning. He had spent over 50 years developing himself every single day. He also commented on how remarkable my success was and asked how I did it. I shared that I studied his books and that "Think and Grow Rich," had drastically changed my life.

Bob gave me one of the books from his own personal library, "Financial Success Through Creative Thought," later named, "The Science of Getting Rich," by Wallace D. Wattles. He told me to never stop studying and to read Chapter 4, ("The First Principle in the Science of Getting Rich"), Chapter 14 ("The Impression of Increase"), and Chapter 7 ("Gratitude"). And to read them in that order.

He told me if I studied those three chapters, in that order for 30 days, my life would change. He was right. In that year, our company grew by over $70 million in sales, and I gave birth to not one but two babies in the last two years.

To say I've been blessed is an understatement.

"Reality is merely an illusion, albeit a very persistent one."

-Albert Einstein

CHAPTER IX:

Escaping the Matrix

I heard it a thousand times: "What you're trying to do is just not realistic." And it wasn't only well-meaning friends telling me that, it was family, too.

Our friends and family mean well, but most of them don't have the experience to draw from when it comes to success. Those that do are probably not successful in the same way you're attempting to be. They see things from their perspective, which in a sense is the absolute truth for them. It's just not your truth.

In my reality anything is possible because nothing is real unless I think it is. Nothing is real unless I accept it. Nothing is what it seems to be, including reality.

Reality is an illusion. A really good one.

What's Real vs. What's Imaginary?

Our reality is all the stuff we can see and touch and taste and hear and smell—the things we perceive to be *real* though our five senses.

There is a scientific theory that suggests that humans don't have five senses, but nine. Other theories say the number is 21, and perhaps as high as 53. So, who's right?

The world around us is far more complicated, mysterious, and magnificent than we realize.

People say to me, "I don't believe in this kind of woo-woo nonsense stuff, I only believe in things I know are real."

Rule:
Have realistic goals.

Reality:
What's realistic is different for each person. Define your own reality.

My response is, "Really, tell me what's real? You mean, like a wall, that kind of real?"

"Yeah, like a wall."

"Because it's solid?" I'll ask.

"Right."

"Well, it's *not* solid—it only *appears* to be solid," I point out. "Even steel isn't really solid. Science has proven that everything is mostly nothing but empty space."

People say they're grounded in reality, but they aren't. They are only grounded in what they *think* is real. The truth is, we live a life of perception.

If you've seen the movie, "The Matrix," you know what I'm talking about.

"The Matrix"

Every now and then, a book or a movie comes along and makes us question our own reality. That's what the movie, "The Matrix," did for millions of people around the world.

The movie is set in a dystopian future where people are unknowingly trapped inside a simulated reality created by intelligent machines that use humans as an energy source. Creepy, right? What's *really* creepy is that it's actually happening to people right now.

Every day, we wake up, get out of bed, and go about our lives accepting things as they are, as we *perceive* them to be, unknowingly trapped inside a system created by people who have figured out how to control others and use their energy for their benefit. We go along, believing in the reality others have created for us.

By the way, the Wachowski brothers, who wrote and directed "The Matrix," were told repeatedly the movie would never work, they would never get it made, it was too far "out there" to be successful. Of course, the movie was an enormous box office hit, grossing $460 million.

The world's attempts to control us is everywhere we look:

- In every commercial, talk show, and newscast on television.

- In every conversation with every friend, family member or coworker.

- In every policy created by the Federal Reserve and every currency issued by every country in the world.

- In every passage in every bible ever written.

- In every political promise ever spoken.

- In celebrity gossip, influencer marketing, and every social media outlet, all of them filled with *other people* telling us what *we* should think, feel, like, and do.

We consume their opinions and think that's how we must feel, because that's how *they* feel and because they're celebrities they must know. We follow and do what they suggest because we want to be like them or be like everybody else because we're so afraid to be different.

This is what holds us back from success. This is what keeps us stuck in the matrix. We sell out our creative force to the cyclical loop of the society designed to keep us trapped.

Create Your Own Truth

The weird people are the people who end up succeeding because they don't care about so-called truths that are blindly accepted by everybody else. They create their own truth. They tune out everything else. This is a secret to success.

Rule:
Society's reality is real.

Reality:
Nothing is as it seems.

We have been blinded from the truth by the very people we trust to tell us the truth. Worse, we let it happen. We buy what they are selling. We have allowed ourselves to become sheep who eagerly let the world pull the wool over our eyes because it's easier than thinking for ourselves and challenging the status quo.

I've always wondered if, at the end of my life, will I be satisfied knowing I gave it my all? Or would I be regretfully upset that I missed the opportunity to leave my mark on the world.

We get so caught up in what everyone else is doing, we completely undermine our own creativity. My thought is, if everyone is doing it, it's probably not the path I want to be on. What everyone else is doing is safe. It's not in my nature to do things out of safety or saving face. In fact, it's way more fun to risk a little (or in my case, a lot) even out of curiosity to see what happens.

People do what everyone else does because they are terrified to trust their inner being. They've been told all their lives what to do and how to do it. They've never once considered trusting themselves for the answers. The interesting thing about humans as a species is that we are multi-dimensional beings.

We are far more powerful than we are taught to believe.

Humans are all connected by the same source of energy and this source of energy allows us to create from our free will. We have the ability to "will things" into existence. If everyone knew they could create what they want in life, there would be no one left in society. Society would collapse. We are witnessing this before our very eyes. What a wild time to be alive. People are at war over the next version of reality. America has even divided itself into two camps.

We have allowed ourselves to make politics the end all be all when we could simply just be governing ourselves. It's almost comical. We are fighting with each other over the illusory two options, Democrat or Republican, not realizing there's an infinite number of possibilities we could choose from. We have let ourselves think small. We have turned over our awareness, our creative life force, and power to a distraction designed to keep us from consciously creating. Those in power do not want you to know this. This is the reason they are successful, and many others are not.

Knowledge isn't power.

Awareness is.

> *Rule:*
> **Don't stand out, blend in. Go with the herd. Do what everyone else is doing.**
>
> *Reality:*
> **Ignore what everyone else is doing and choose to create a custom life.**

When you begin to awaken to this information, you will never let anyone create your life for you, ever again.

Life becomes fun when you refuse to lock your mind up with anything other than what you are choosing to create.

Escaping the Matrix

The real matrix is everything holding you back from your dream life. It's the rules you're following that you wish you could break. During my own pursuit of happiness, I became painstakingly aware of all the things I needed to let go of. Fear, being at the top of that list, and following other people's rules.

I began questioning everything I thought was true. Every supposed fact and truth, every rule, guideline, and restriction. I consciously decided whether or not I'd accept it as a truth and if I'd follow it.

Nothing I believed or thought I believed to that point was off limits.

To truly escape the matrix, you must be willing to leave normal behind. You cannot become extraordinary in your life if you never leave your comfort zone. Nothing great comes from comfort zones.

What is holding you back from escaping your matrix?

Is it your job? Your spouse? Money? Your friends and family? Your religious beliefs? Identify what is currently blocking you from the life you would choose to live if you knew you could live it.

Whatever is holding you back, you must choose to succeed anyway. You can escape your matrix. You just have to choose to redefine the rules you're following and living by.

The Two Pills

In "The Matrix," the main character Neo gets to see the world for what it really is. He gets to see the truth. He's being used. He is a pawn in someone else's game. But he is given a choice between taking a blue pill or a red pill.

The blue pill will let him go back to the false life he had been living. An unconscious life spent stumbling around in the dark, controlled by outside forces who are using him for their purposes. All he must do is take the blue pill and he'll be plugged back into the matrix, back in his old life.

Taking the red pill would let Neo stay and see reality for what it truly is—a magnificent place where people can create their own path through intentional awareness.

It's a big choice.

One path is easy because all he has to do is numb himself with distractions and surrender his freedom. The other path is hard.

The other path requires courage and personal responsibility. It requires that he fight the system, one that is designed for him to fail. This path requires him to wake up from society's deep sleep.

Our Most Sacred Privilege

The question every person needs to answer is: Whose reality do I want to live in? One of my own making or someone else's? It is perhaps the most sacred choice we will ever make.

Rule:
It's important to have a firm grasp on reality.

Reality:
Successful people create their own reality.

Should I just keep going along like a leaf drifting aimlessly down a river, out of control, at the mercy of the current? Or do I dare go my own way, awake and aware on a more challenging but rewarding path, governed by rules of my own making?

Neo took the red pill. So did I.

*"How wonderful it is that nobody need wait a
single moment before starting to improve the
world."*

-Anne Frank

CHAPTER X:

HempWorx

I first started showing signs of illness in 2014 just as MyDailyChoice was launching. Josh and I were working long hours to get the business to where we knew it could be. We traveled back and forth from Maryland to Vegas to attend networking events before finally, in early 2016, deciding to move there.

By the time we arrived in Vegas, my health was severely impacted. My hair was falling out, and my skin was a mess. I was so tired, I could barely function.

I've always thought of myself as the strongest person I know, but I was falling apart. Physically. Emotionally. Mentally. Spiritually. I said, "God, if you're out there, show me a sign."

The doctors diagnosed me with celiac disease, a rare autoimmune disease triggered by eating gluten (wheat, barley, rye). I cut gluten out of my diet as they recommended, but I wasn't getting any better. My body was not absorbing nutrients. The only thing the doctors said they could do was to keep running tests.

One day, I was sitting in the doctor's office, waiting to go in for my appointment, and began researching natural remedies for celiac disease. The first article that popped up was about cannabis.

The article said cannabis could cure celiac. I remember thinking, "What am I doing here? These tests are getting me nowhere." I stood up and headed to the door. I was off to get my medical marijuana card.

Learning About CBD Oil

I went to a medical marijuana doctor to apply for my card. I had no history or experience with marijuana. I didn't even know the difference between marijuana and hemp at the time.

I was on the fourth day of a migraine when my medical marijuana card arrived. I went straight to the dispensary and started learning about all the different options available to me. I decided to try CBD (Cannabidiol).

At first, after I started taking it, I wasn't all that impressed. There were no noticeable results. I didn't have any life-changing experience. Maybe CBD wasn't the answer.

A month or two after first trying it, Josh found a farm in Kentucky that was growing hemp to extract CBD. They asked if we wanted to try some samples of their CBD oil. I said absolutely. At that point I was willing to try just about anything.

Within seven days, my symptoms begin to reverse, and I felt normal for the first time in many years. Then I wondered if it was just a placebo effect. I knew the mind had the ability to impact the body in many ways, both positive and negative, and anything was possible.

I decided the best test was to give the product to others, starting with friends and family, to see if they had the same experience I had. They all came back with positive results. Not only had this CBD oil transformed my life, but it was also changing other people's lives too.

Because of my personal health turnaround, I told Josh we should make CBD oil part of the MyDailyChoice product line. He was less than enthusiastic.

Seeing Down the Road

Josh has always been something of a whiz kid. By the age of 14 he was ranked #23 in the world by The United States Chess Federation.

I have played chess with Josh, but I've never beat him. Not many people have. He tries to teach me, but I do not have the patience to learn it.

Rule:
There is a perfect time for everything.

Reality:
There is rarely a perfect time for anything.

Anyone who knows anything about playing chess will tell you the key to winning is having the ability to see what is going to happen before it does. I could see that adding a CBD oil line to the company would be a huge success, but even as a world class chess player, Josh did not. He told me no. So, I decided to do it outside of MyDailyChoice. When I told Josh my plans, he asked what I was going to call it. I told him, "HempWorx, because our hemp *works*."

Launching HempWorx

HempWorx is a play on words: Hemp, which describes the fiber of the cannabis plant from which CBD oil is extracted, and Worx, as in DreamWorks because it works. It did not take long to come up with the name, either. To be quite honest, at the time I was completely high (on "medical" marijuana of course), or as I like to say, I was tapped into my "higher" consciousness. No other names were considered. When something is perfect, you just know it.

The biggest hurdle was money. Josh's funds were completely committed to keeping MyDailyChoice in business, and there was nothing to spare as it was still in its infancy. In addition, with Hemp Worx being my company, there was no way Josh was going to promote another company as the CEO of MyDailyChoice. With this venture, I was truly on my own—but Josh *did* agree to help me get things up and running.

Maybe I was naïve to think Josh and I could pull it off. I guess deep down, I knew we could. It felt right. I felt like I was for once in my life, in complete alignment with my purpose. I was meant to bring these products to the masses. I just had to do my part.

I was determined to make HempWorx successful even if I did not know exactly how it was all going to work. In this case, my naïveté turned out to be a strength, not a weakness. All the personal development I had done had started to take hold, and I was confident enough to know it was possible.

There is a saying that I love in network marketing: "Ignorance on fire beats knowledge on ice." I was so passionate about these products and how they changed my life, I knew other people needed them, too. I had a clear vision of where we were heading despite not knowing exactly how to get there. Both Josh and I were determined to figure things out.

Doing Everything Myself

Since I didn't have money to invest in hiring a graphic designer, I created the logo and the branding for HempWorx myself. To save time and money, we used a regular Shopify website (that later got flagged for selling cannabis and was shut down). I put together the bare minimums for starting an online business.

I announced on Facebook that I was going to be selling CBD products to consumers. Initially, there was no affiliate referral option. I started a Facebook group that quickly grew to 100,000 in just eight short weeks. I spent hours every day, educating people by doing live videos, creating marketing materials, and answering thousands of comments and messages. I was in the trenches. It was hard work, but it was the first time in my life where I felt like I was creating positive impact and change in the world. People were getting results. Hundreds and then thousands of lives were changed for the better. No matter how exhausting the late hours were, I knew it was my mission to deliver wellness and healing to the people. I was so sick for so long. CBD saved me. It saved many.

Rule:
The purpose of business is to turn a profit.

Reality:
Profit is the by-product of delivering value to others.

I was getting hundreds of testimonials from people who loved the product. HempWorx went from 5 orders to 100 orders a day, then quickly to 200 orders a day.

HempWorx had gone from a simple idea, backed by belief and desire, to a movement overnight. I had enough proof for Josh to see this was going to be big.

I went back to Josh and I said, "The people have spoken. They want CBD. Can we merge our companies together so that HempWorx becomes a brand in MyDailyChoice?"

He agreed.

The sheer number of orders received in such a short period of time was proof that my intuition was correct. People were ready for hemp-based products. There was no way Josh could argue with the results.

Eight short weeks after I launched HempWorx, we made the decision to merge. I was still functioning as an affiliate inside MyDailyChoice, with a large team there, a role I was unwilling to relinquish. My heart was still very much in the field. But I was also the founder of HempWorx. I decided to assume responsibility for both roles.

Interestingly, this was also a bit of a rule-breaking move in the industry. To be an affiliate and be a part of corporate is something that typically doesn't happen. However, in this scenario, it made sense.

Safe Is Risky

Early on in the CBD movement, there was no clarity on what was legal and what wasn't. HempWorx was riding on the tails of the outdated 2014 Farm Bill, which made it highly risky at the time. (The issue regarding legality was resolved when the Farm Bill was signed into law by President Trump in 2018, defining hemp as legal and separate from marijuana.) If we had waited for this to happen before launching HempWorx, it would have been too late. Other CBD companies were being shut down. These companies didn't have a Josh Zwagil.

Rule:
The prudent thing is to 'play it safe.'

Reality:
In a world that is moving fast, playing it safe is the riskiest thing you can do.

By the end of 2017, sales hit $9.7 million. The following year, we'd become the fastest growing network marketing company in the industry, 10Xing our sales to $100 million. In 2019, MyDailyChoice and HempWorx reached $170 million in sales. Record-breaking growth year after year.

It was risky starting HempWorx. But there is always a risk in *not* taking risks. Choose your risk.

In my case, it may have been a gut feeling, higher power, or some unknown form of internal guidance—whatever it was, this I knew: When that tiny voice says you need to do something, listen.

"I battled my past, my weaknesses, and society's attempt to control me since the day I was born. Some say that makes me a survivor, I say it makes me a conqueror."

-Jenna Zwagil

CHAPTER XI:

Rebel With a Cause

When I was a kid, I was always pushing my boundaries. Mainly out of curiosity. I wanted to know what happened when you took that path. I questioned if my parents really knew what they were doing. I thought I had a better chance at just listening to myself. I never meant any disrespect to them; I just wasn't interested in doing things their way and my freedom was worth putting up a fight.

Even as a young adult, I lived my life recklessly. No one could have talked any sense into me. I took it quite literally that, when you turn 18 you get to do whatever you want. I had been waiting for this ability my whole childhood. With that said, I didn't waste any time getting into the thick of it. Married at 18, became a mom by 19. Divorced twice and had two kids by 24. Suicidal by age 30. Multi-millionaire and top woman in the network marketing and cannabis industries by age 33. I didn't waste any time getting started at life. I lived fast and furiously and made hundreds of mistakes. I failed over and over again. It led me to success.

If you keep failing, you keep moving forward. You are learning. You're figuring things out. You're getting closer. I lived my early life spiraling in the cosmos, out of control. My subconscious mind was still programmed by society / the matrix and I hadn't yet figured out how to program myself.

As I arrived at rock bottom after spinning out for several years, I realized I could have taken back control sooner, had I only known I was in the driver's seat the whole time and all I had to do was WAKE UP. I was fighting myself. I was rebelling against this systemic conformity and didn't know why. After learning how to program myself, success was there, waiting.

Today, I have finally arrived at a place where I break rules for conscientious reasons: to make the world a better place and to enrich the lives of others. It was a long road that took three decades and thousands of hours of study and self-work.

James Dean said, "Life is short, break the rules." In his case, life was especially short. But the world remembers him all these years later. Why? Because he was a rule-breaker.

One of James Dean's most iconic films was called, "Rebel Without a Cause." What a sad thought, to be a rebel with no reason. The world wouldn't be what it is today without people going against the status quo and societal norms. Entrepreneurs who leave their jobs and sense of safety behind to pursue their higher purpose are rebels. They are fighting to break out of the system, to escape the rat race, to live life on their terms. My underlying cause for rebellion both as a child and adult was freedom. Financial freedom. Freedom from unnecessary rules and restrictions. I just wanted to live my life the way I wanted to live my life and as I grew up, I realized that *that* would be a whole mission to accomplish.

Being a Rebel <u>with</u> a Cause

People who break rules simply to be rule breakers are soon forgotten because society never benefits from selfish rebellion. But when people break rules for the right reasons, for the good of society, they often make history. There's a big difference between being a rule breaker *just because* and being a rule breaker *for a cause.* Effective rebellion always has a purpose behind it.

Rule:
Money is the greatest motivator.

My life changed so drastically from using CBD, that I did not care if I made money from the busines. I was so excited to share these products with the world because watching people get better, like myself, was the real reward.

Reality:
The ultimate motivator is changing lives.

Zig Ziglar was famous for saying, "You can have everything in life you want if you will just help other people get what they want." Our business is driven by this philosophy.

I just want to be remembered by the positive impact I have created in other people lives. Adding value to people is what gets me up in the morning, it's what keeps me going. If I had had a mentor earlier in my life, I could have avoided some of the toughest challenges I experienced. Had I had someone like me to wake me up from my unconsciousness, I could have helped impact the world sooner. My goal is to help people wake up sooner, so that they, too, can fulfill their purpose. I want to be remembered for that.

Be Yourself

Successful network marketers will tell you that if you want to be successful, you have to change who you are. And I admit, when I first started, I bought into a lot of it. I thought creating your brand and image first would lead to success because if I appeared to be successful, I would become successful. If I dressed a certain way, spoke a certain way, avoided controversy, and was ALWAYS positive, I'd be successful, eventually. I was wrong. I became successful while still being an imperfectly unscripted me.

I am proof that you can still be *you* and also succeed. The world needs fewer Hollywood idols and more real people winning. I want to live in a world where the expression of our individuality is celebrated, not ridiculed. Being unapologetically you is your contribution to the world, not something to hide from it. You never know who you will inspire to pursue their purpose. You will make success believable and if more people believe they can be successful, the more successful people there will be.

Be you. Be the best *you* that you can be, and you will light the path for others to do the same.

When I got into the network marketing industry, people told me to change. Now they tell me to never change. That is the result of pursuing purpose while staying committed to my true self. Being yourself is an act of rebellion, and it's one that's worth the risk.

"Well-behaved women seldom make history."
-Eleanor Roosevelt

CHAPTER XII:

Why I Wrote This Book

Most people know me through social media. That is where I got my start and where I had the opportunity to build thousands of relationships and connections with people in a short amount of time. While I have been effective at sharing my story through posts, live videos, and one-on-one zoom calls, I wanted to create a bigger impact by putting it all down in one place. I wrote this book on the off chance my story makes a difference to people who are ready to grow and become their best selves. Even if you're in a different business or industry than me, I hope this book helps you in some way. I don't care what you choose to do with your life so long as you decide to do something with passion and purpose.

Life Is Filled With Challenges

I still remember the very first opportunity meeting we held for MyDailyChoice in Baltimore. Only 14 people showed up. I thought, "This is going to be harder than I thought. This is going to be a challenge." I was right. It was.

But you know what? Life is supposed to be challenging. The world is our classroom, a stage we learn to play the game of life on.

Josh and I still face challenges, like anyone does with any business, but we aren't stopped by them anymore. We know challenges are what teaches us how to get to the next level. Without challenge, no change can happen. Instead of avoiding challenges, we must embrace them. They are how we grow and continue to get better.

Control Your Destiny

We must consciously choose to change our future by agreeing to stop reliving the past. To control your destiny, you must control your mind and focus only on where you want to go. I have no desire to simply go through the motions, I want to *grow* through life. You have the ability to achieve everything you want to if your vision is clear and backed by massive belief and action.

Rule:
Your destiny is prewritten.

Reality:
You are the author of your destiny.

The Power of Belief

As badly as I wanted to succeed early in my life, I simply didn't believe I could do it. In that regard, Josh saw my future before I did. He believed in me when I didn't. He cheered me on when I wouldn't. He saw the greatness in me before I saw it in myself and spoke life into the dreams that at one point I was too afraid to believe in.

Sometimes we need to borrow belief from someone who can see our greatness before we can, when it's hard for us to believe that we're capable of success.

I don't have all the answers to being a great leader, but I do know it's important to believe in people and cast a vision for them when they can't see it for themselves.

I'd been married twice before, but Josh was the first person who inspired me to create positive change within myself. One person can change your reality. In my case, that person was Josh. And I thank him for having faith in me and for taking my wild ideas seriously.

I wrote this book so my story could live on and inspire people for years to come. The other reason I wrote this book is because I have faith in you. Even if we've never met and I know absolutely nothing about you, I have faith in you.

Why?

Because every person on this planet has unlimited potential to achieve virtually any goal and create the life they desire.

You have the ability to create the life you desire.

Permission to Succeed

The final reason I wrote this book is to get you prepared for the road ahead. Success is not for the timid, it's for people who buckle up and take action.

Josh cheered me on and encouraged me to become who I was meant to be, and for that I will be forever grateful. But as important as that was, *I did the work.*

There will be work involved. There is no way around it.

Nothing of value is achieved through inaction. Some of that action should include a close look at the rules you've been following—in some cases for your entire life. Ask yourself, "Does this rule make sense? Does following it empower me to become the person I am meant to be? Will continuing to follow it lead me to the life I want for myself and my family?"

There are some people who have become so obedient to following the rules society places on us that breaking the rules is uncomfortable and not always supported by friends and family.

Maybe you're waiting for someone to give you permission to break the rules, even though no permission is required. So, in the words of Robert Hollis, eight-figure income-earner with over 30 years in the network marketing industry, "If no one has given you permission to succeed, let me be the first."

You have permission.

Now get busy.

Declaring Your Intentions to the Universe

The following four "Quick Start Steps" are designed to get you started down the path to the life *you* want, not the one other people have planned for you:

1... Visualize your dream life:

Who do you want to become? What are your goals to tackle upon finishing this book? Do you want to become the next big leader in network marketing? Do you want to quit your job and live your passion roaming the Earth in an RV? Do you want to un-school your kids and take back the choice to educate them with real-world experiences vs. classroom indoctrination? Do you imagine having an off-grid homestead where you can grow your own food and become truly self-sufficient? Or, do you want to have millions in the bank and live a lavish lifestyle?

2... Write it down!

Whatever your goals are and your vision for your future, WRITE THEM DOWN (in present tense). DO NOT SKIP THIS STEP. When we take the time to truly visualize our dreams and physically write them on paper, we are taking an idea from the creative, formless substance and bringing it into our physical reality.

EXAMPLE: "I no longer work a 9-5 job. I'm happy to now be living on my 50-acre homestead, working just a few hours a day making $100,000 a month. With this money, I am able to not only support my family but also donate to people in need. I wake up every day full of excitement and passion. I am grateful for all I have achieved. (Be very specific!)

3... Post it where you can see it:

After you've written it down, do it again; make two copies of it. Put one in your wallet and post one up on your bathroom mirror or somewhere you will see it every day. Read it three times a day until it's manifested. (Read it with conviction!)

4... Post it on social media:

Post it on Facebook, Instagram or other social media outlet of your choice and use the hashtag: #BreakingAllTheRules

A year from now it'll show up in your memories, and you will have already achieved it or will be much closer. This creates accountability among your friends and followers and helps get things into motion.

Connect With Me:

- **Facebook FAN PAGE @officialjennaz**
- **Instagram @officialjennaZ**

About the Author...

Jenna Zwagil grew up in a dusty little town in the inland deserts of California. She bounced around from one meaningless job to another and, from all outside appearances, had few prospects for a successful life. But Jenna had a burning desire to do and be more. Her senior yearbook 10-year prediction was: ***Retired as a Business Owner.***

The only problem was she hadn't figured out what that business was supposed to be. Even as obstacles piled up around her as fast as her debt, she didn't give up. Then, during the summer of 2014, Jenna met Josh Zwagil, who was about to launch MyDailyChoice (aka, MDC) a net-work marketing company. Jenna joined as one of the first affiliates.

After three rollercoaster years in the MDC start-up, Jenna discovered CBD oil and was convinced that it was not only a product she needed but something that the market needed, as well. She called it HempWorx, and it turns our she was right. The market for their product was ready to explode.

MDC merged with HempWorx in 2017. Jenna and Josh also merged their relationship as husband and wife. Today, they are at the helm of a multi-million-dollar business. MDC hit $100 million in sales in 2018 and continues to grow year after year.

Beyond her work inside the company, Jenna has a passion for mentorship. She loves sharing the hard-fought lessons she's learned both on her personal journey and through reading and studying the greatest personal development teachers of all time, such as Napoleon Hill, Bob Proctor, Eckhart Tolle, and many others. Jenna resides in Las Vegas with her husband and business partner, Josh, and their four kids.

Made in the USA
Coppell, TX
12 March 2021